THE **LOO**
COMPANION

Surrey-based author **Mark Leigh** has written or co-written thirty-nine humour and trivia books, many of which have pride of place in other people's toilets.

He has worked with the Great & the Good including Jeremy Beadle, Julian Clary, Rolf Harris, Ade Edmondson, Des Lynam, Pamela Stephenson and even Roy Chubby Brown. TV projects have included writing for Hale & Pace, Russ Abbot, Brian Conley, Jimmy Tarbuck, Rory Bremner, Noel Edmonds and Bobby Davro (a dark period in his life of which he is truly ashamed). Works in progress include a comedy novel *Dick Longg Saves the World!* and various spec film scripts.

Mark has been going to the toilet since a very early age.

For more details visit **www.mark-leigh.com**

THE LOO COMPANION

ARE YOU SITTING COMFORTABLY?

MARK LEIGH

Michael O'Mara Books Limited

First published in Great Britain in 2011 by
Michael O'Mara Books Limited
9 Lion Yard
Tremadoc Road
London SW4 7NQ

A CIP catalogue record for this book is available from the British Library.

Papers used by Michael O'Mara Books Limited are natural, recyclable products made from wood grown in sustainable forests. The manufacturing processes conform to the environmental regulations of the country of origin.

ISBN: 978-1-84317-631-2

7 8 9 10

www.mombooks.com

Cover design by Allan Somerville

Designed and typeset by K DESIGN, Winscombe, Somerset

Printed and bound by CPI Group (UK) Ltd, Croydon, CR0 4YY

Introduction

Those who are aware of the quality of my writing and my back catalogue know that when the idea of a book all about toilets and toilet-related activity first comes up, I am the obvious 'go-to guy'. I was proud to receive the commission to write *The Loo Companion*; however, having to deliver approximately thirty thousand words on the subject was an extremely daunting prospect – the equivalent of writing a whole dissertation on the world of U-bends, urine and poop.

It was with this heightened sense of trepidation that I embarked upon my research. But it soon became apparent that the topic was as fascinating as it was repellent. Before long I'd totally immersed myself in toilets. I found myself caring about the khazi and growing fond of flushing. In essence, I'd fallen in love with the loo.

The deeper I delved, the more I became mesmerized. The subject was as absorbing as three-ply toilet paper and just as important. After all, it's said that civilization did not begin with the wheel but with the toilet. It was this invention that enabled early man to stop wandering around aimlessly looking for somewhere new to take a dump and instead settle down, build a society and invent stuff (like the wheel, for example). The fact that the Inuits have twelve words for snow but we have over fifty different euphemisms for crapping, many quite hilarious, just illustrates how important the toilet is in our lives.

We each spend three years of our lives sitting on one (more if we're constipated) and it's humbling to think that the smallest room in the house has been the place of birth and death of statesmen, royalty and celebrities – Judy Garland, Lenny Bruce and Elvis Presley to name but three who died with their trousers around their ankles (although I'm not sure if Judy Garland was actually wearing trousers at the time).

In the course of my studies I stumbled across facts like the anxiety of peeing in public is second only to the fear of public speaking, that the odds of receiving a toilet-related injury are 1 in 10,000, that Simon Cowell once called a *Britain's Got Talent* contestant who farted 'The Blue Danube' 'a vile, disgusting creature' and that most toilets flush in the key of E flat.

But before you join me in unravelling the rich tapestry that is the toilet, let me leave you with a small piece of philosophy that was given to me by a wise old man I met in South China's Yunnan province during the course of my research:

'May your life be like toilet paper. Long and useful.'

Mark Leigh, Surrey, England 2011

Acknowledgements

A big thank you to the following people, who either contributed helpful ideas for this book, lent me their laptop or just stayed out of my way while I was writing (you know which category you fall into):

Melanie Hammerton

Graham Hart

Sara Howell

Darin Jewell

Neville Landau

Debbie, Polly and Barney Leigh

Philip Leigh

Anna Marx

John and Lesley Wright.

'Passing gas is necessary to well-being.'

HIPPOCRATES

Toilet humour 1

A Native American Chief walks into a trading post and asks for toilet paper. The clerk says he has three types for sale: unbranded, Andrex or White Cloud.

'White Cloud sounds like good, trustworthy Indian toilet paper,' says the Chief. 'How much is it?'

'$2.00 a roll,' the clerk replies.

'That's a lot of money,' the Chief replies. 'What about the others?'

'Andrex is $1.00 a roll and the unbranded type is 40 cents a roll.'

The Chief doesn't have much cash but he looks in his money pouch and manages to find 40 cents for the unbranded type.

Within a few hours he's back at the trading post, throwing the roll he just bought back at the clerk.

'This cheap toilet paper is useless!', he announces. 'It is so useless that I have given it a brand name,' he angrily tells the clerk. 'From now on I shall call it John Wayne.'

'Why John Wayne?' asks the confused clerk.

'Because it's rough and it's tough and it won't take no crap off an Indian.'

Before toilet paper . . .

Prior to the soft, perforated paper we take for granted today, different civilizations used a wide variety of materials:

VIKINGS: discarded sheep and lambs wool

ANCIENT GREEKS: smooth stones

ROMANS: a sponge soaked in salt water on the end of a stick (wealthy Romans, however, used a wool pad rather than a sponge, and rosewater)

NOMADIC ARABS and other desert dwellers: sand

MEDIEVAL COMMONERS: straw, hay or grass

MEDIEVAL RULING CLASSES: wool or hemp

EARLY AMERICAN SETTLERS: rags, newsprint, corncobs or leaves

HAWAIIAN NATIVES: pieces of coconut shell husk

INUITS: snow and tundra moss

MEDIEVAL MONKS: pottery shards

THE COURT OF LOUIS XIV: lace

Did you know?

Psycho **was the first studio movie to show a toilet flushing on screen. At the time the scene caused a huge outcry and a deluge of complaints about indecency.**

Privy Playtime:
Toilet **True** or F**alse**?

Answers can be found at the rear end of the book.

1. During Operation Desert Storm in 1991 the US military didn't have time to camouflage all their tanks before they were deployed in the desert so they draped them in toilet paper.

2. In Japan you can buy edible toilet paper that comes in three exotic fruit flavours.

3. The Sultan of Brunei has a gold-plated toilet that flushes Evian water.

4. To discourage intravenous drug abuse some public toilets are bathed in a cool blue light . . . this makes it difficult for users to detect veins.

5. When Native Americans first saw a western toilet they called it 'The China Throne of the Great White God'.

6. The *Farmers' Almanac* publication used to be produced with a hole in one corner because the publishers knew it would eventually be hung from an outhouse wall.

7. In North Korea, farting in public is punishable by a fine of the equivalent of £220.

8 At the end of the eighteenth century, toilets were more popular among the Maoris in New Zealand than they were in London.

9 Albert Einstein came up with his theory of relativity while seated on the toilet.

10 Hong Kong jewellers Hang Fung have a 24K gold-plated toilet worth $5 million.

11 After his death Adolf Hitler's last turd was retrieved from his Berlin bunker by US soldiers and until it was destroyed in a fire, was on show in a New Jersey Museum of Oddities.

12 In warfare, forces retreating from a town often smash toilets to frustrate the advancing enemy forces.

13 The Yanomami, a South American Indian tribe, use farting as a form of greeting.

14 The toilet in Prince Philip's private bathroom at Sandringham plays the first bars of 'God Save The Queen' when the lid is lifted.

15 Designed to be installed in an office, a machine in Japan can turn used photocopier paper into toilet rolls.

16 Toilet rolls were used as a form of currency in war-torn Mogadishu.

That's just gross!

☞ **In an emergency (and I mean *real* emergency) urine can be used as a laxative. Drinking it on an empty stomach can stimulate diarrhoea.**

No more yellow snow

Europe's highest toilets have been built on the peak of the continent's tallest peak, Mont Blanc in France. More than thirty thousand people visit the peak each year and, according to local mayor Jean-Marc Peillex, the toilets are 'much needed'. He commented, 'Our beautiful mountain's white peak was full of yellow and brown spots in summer'. The two toilets were helicoptered up Mont Blanc to a height of approx. 14,000 feet (4260 m). Helicopters will also be used to remove waste from the toilets on a daily basis at the peak's busiest times.

NB At the announcement about the toilets someone asked whether, if one of these helicopters crashed, the shit would hit the fan.

Did you know?

Before toilet paper, sailors were in the habit of using the frayed end of an old anchor rope ... and yes, they all shared the same rope.

Welcome to the Loo-vre

The smallest art gallery in the world is believed to be the Bog Standard Gallery, created in 2007 by British artist Melanie Warner. The 1 m² gallery space was created in an old Portaloo and recently received its fifty thousandth visitor.

Former Manchester Metropolitan University art student Melanie, twenty-two, bought the worn-out lavatory from a hire firm for £125 and then spent six weeks converting it into her gallery. After removing the seat and plumbing, she painted the walls bright white, installed an oak floor and a skylight. On display is an assortment of six hundred photos of toilet signs from around the world, taken during holidays abroad.

> 'Never kick a fresh turd on a hot day.'
> HARRY S. TRUMAN

A toilet by any other name

The ancient Israelites referred to the room containing a toilet as 'The House of Honour', while to the ancient Egyptians it was 'The House of the Morning'. Other quaint names throughout history include the 'Necessarium' (literally, the necessary house), the 'Reredorter' (the room at the rear of a dormitory), the 'Adornment Place', the 'Best Room' and, of course, the 'Privy' (the private place).

NB The word 'toilet' is actually a euphemism itself. Originally the word just meant the process of washing and dressing as in 'the lady has just completed her toilet' and didn't enter common use before the 1830s.

Privy Playtime:
Closet Sudoku

The solution can be found at the rear end of the book.

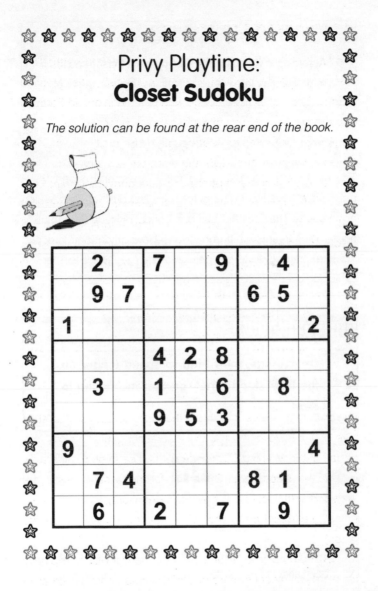

	2		7		9		4	
	9	7				6	5	
1								2
			4	2	8			
	3		1		6		8	
			9	5	3			
9								4
	7	4				8	1	
	6		2		7		9	

A penny for your thoughts . . .

The euphemism for using the toilet, 'to spend a penny', is believed to have its origins in the very first public toilets, which appeared at The Crystal Palace in London's Hyde Park (built to house The Great Exhibition of 1851). Here, attendants dressed in white charged visitors a penny to use the facilities. After the exhibition over 820,000 visitors had used the toilets.

Did you know?

On average, men tend to spend longer on the toilet due to their greater inclination to read.

Toilet humour 2

A construction worker goes to his doctor and says, 'Doc, you've got to help me. I am so constipated.' He drops his trousers and pants.

The doctor examines him and then says, 'Lean over the table.'

The construction worker does what he's told and, without warning, the doctor whacks him on the arse with a baseball bat and then tells him to use the bathroom.

He comes out a few minutes later with a relieved look and says, 'Doc, I've just shat for the first time in weeks. I feel great. What can I do to stop the constipation returning?'

The doctor says, 'Stop wiping with old cement bags.'

Carry on Up The Toilet

British actor and 'Carry On' star Kenneth Willams constantly suffered from piles and refused to use other people's toilets – or let anyone else use his. Whenever he visited theatres he always insisted on taking his own personal toilet paper and any visitors to his home in London's West End had to use the toilet at the nearby Tottenham Court Road tube station.

Not sitting comfortably

A South African woman, Susanna Jacoba de Beer, successfully sued the South African Ministry of Defence for £7,000 following injuries sustained when a toilet collapsed at a military hospital in Pretoria in 1999. The incident occurred when she was visiting her husband, a retired soldier. In her submission to the court, Mrs de Beer said that seconds after she sat down the toilet bowl shattered beneath her. She landed on broken pieces of the bowl and remains scarred from the incident.

Did you know?

Prisoners used to mix their urine with coal dust to make a tattoo dye.

Open wide!

Thirty-five-year-old Matthew Walton, a dentist from Shrewsbury, was struck off by the General Dental Council (GDC) in March 2011 after charges were brought against him of farting in front of patients and staff. One of his nurses, Carol Stokes, told the hearing how she begged the dentist to stop: 'It was annoying. I didn't like the smell around the practice and it made us feel sick.'

Walton admitted that he did have 'inadvertent' outbreaks of flatulence and admitted that a colleague once had to spray air freshener to cover the smell. The GDC ruled that his conduct required immediate suspension of his registration, 'for the protection of the public'.

At the time of writing it is unclear whether Mr Walton is going to appeal.

❖ ❖ ❖ ❖ ❖ ❖ ❖ ❖ ❖ ❖ ❖ ❖ ❖ ❖ ❖ ❖ ❖

Toilet humour **3**

Johnny's teacher asks, 'Johnny, give me a sentence with the word "definitely" in it.'

The colour drains from Johnny's face and he gingerly asks, 'Miss, are farts squidgy and lumpy?'

The teacher's confused by this question but answers, 'Of course not Johnny.'

Johnny gulps and replies, 'In that case, Miss, I have definitely shat my pants.'

❖ ❖ ❖ ❖ ❖ ❖ ❖ ❖ ❖ ❖ ❖ ❖ ❖ ❖ ❖ ❖ ❖

Statistically speaking

According to a survey undertaken by the Scott Paper Company, the better educated you are, the more likely you are going to read in the bathroom. Fifty per cent of high school degrees admitted reading on the toilet. This figure increased to 56 per cent of college graduates and 67 per cent of those with a masters degree or doctorate.

Apollonius woz 'ere

The oldest surviving graffiti is thought to be that on a wall in the city of Herculaneum that was buried by ash from the eruption of Mount Vesuvius in AD 79. It reads, 'Apollonius medicus titi imp. Hic cacarit bene', which roughly translates as, 'Apollonius, doctor of Emperor Titus, had a good crap here'.

WC chant

The crude toilets in Korean monasteries often have mantras written on their walls. One to chant on entering the toilet is: 'To eliminate, and eliminate again, is such a joy! May I eliminate the three poisons avarice, anger and foolishness in the same way, so that I become, in an instant, free from wrongdoing.' Say this three times.

Did you know?

The first recorded toilet air fresheners were pomegranates studded with cloves.

No. 2 listed

According to Birmingham Council's Head of Conservation, a Grade II-listed toilet in Court Road, Balsall Heath is 'probably the most magnificent toilet we have got'. This 1890 toilet, which, because of its status, cannot be demolished or altered, features 'decorated panels of geometric and scrolled grotesque patterns'.

What's in a name?

Puddletown in Dorset, England, was originally known as Piddletown, but changed its name with effect from 1 October 1929, many believe as a result of local sensibilities.

Interestingly, it's just a few miles from the village of Shitterton at nearby Bere Regis.

We are not amused . . .

Queen Victoria was being shown around Cambridge University at a time when the town sewers discharged directly into the River Cam. She turned to her guide Dr Whewell, Master of Trinity, and asked what all the pieces of paper floating on the surface were. Not wanting to admit to Her Majesty that they were pieces of toilet paper he calmly replied, 'Ma'am, they are notices to say that bathing is forbidden.'

Bravo Poo Zero

Members of the elite SAS defecate into plastic bags that are then sealed and carried in their rucksacks until they can be safely disposed of. They can't take the chance of an enemy finding and analysing their faeces to discover what they've been eating and, therefore, from where they have travelled.

'Work hard, trust in God, and keep your bowels open.'
OLIVER CROMWELL

Toilet humour 4

An old woman is in a lift in a department store when three young, stylish and very beautiful women get in. All look condescendingly at the old woman, then the first one sprays herself with perfume and announces arrogantly, 'Chanel No. 5, £400 per ounce'.

The next young woman takes out her perfume and sprays herself saying, 'Notorious by Ralph Lauren, £700 per ounce'.

The last young woman does the same, saying, 'Eau de Parfum by Bulgari, £900 per ounce'.

Just before she gets out at her floor the old woman lifts up one leg, farts and announces, 'Cabbage, 60p a pound'.

Credit where credit's due

The flushing toilet was not, as most people believe, invented by Thomas Crapper. It was actually developed in 1596 (or 1592 according to some records), nearly 250 years before he lived, by Sir John Harington, a visionary British nobleman and godson of Queen Elizabeth I. Harington developed a new type of valve that, when pulled, would release water from a 'water closet' to flush any waste products away. Harington installed a flush toilet for Queen Elizabeth I at Richmond Palace, although she is said not to have used it because it made far too much noise. The design was way ahead of its time and was not adopted on a wide scale in England but became far more popular in France. (Harington called his device the Ajax, a play on the words 'A jakes', jakes being an old slang word for a latrine).

Thomas Crapper (1836–1910) had a successful career in the plumbing industry and did much to popularize the use of the toilet, holding nine patents and developing some important related inventions, including the floating ball cock and the pull-chain system for flushing. American and Canadian soldiers stationed in England during World War I used his name as a euphemism for the toilet when they returned home.

❖ ❖ ❖ ❖ ❖ ❖ ❖ ❖ ❖ ❖ ❖ ❖ ❖ ❖ ❖ ❖ ❖

Toilet humour 5

Q: What two words will vacate a men's public toilet?

A: Nice dick!

❖ ❖ ❖ ❖ ❖ ❖ ❖ ❖ ❖ ❖ ❖ ❖ ❖ ❖ ❖ ❖ ❖

Statistically speaking

On average it takes seventy-one visits to the bathroom to use up a complete toilet roll.

Peeing if you're posh

If you're ever in the presence of the Queen and feel the need to relieve yourself, it's important to know the appropriate word to use. Use the wrong word and your poor breeding will be evident, as Carole Middleton, mother to Catherine, now Duchess of Cambridge, found to her horror in April 2007. According to an article in *The Independent*, a Royal Insider described her as 'pushy, rather twee and incredibly middle class' and, as a result, ignorant of the ways to behave in the presence of people too posh to have to work.

So what was her invidious crime? She used the word 'toilet'. The socially acceptable word to use within such company is lavatory or loo – even 'bog' would have been suitable – but never, ever toilet.

Did you know?

St Augustine recognized the ability to fart at will for entertainment purposes as early as the fifth century. In *The City of God* he mentions men who 'have such command of their bowels that they can break wind continuously at will, so as to produce the effect of singing'.

Beats for the bathroom

As a musical accompaniment to your bathroom business, how about selecting one of these toilet tracks?

'Anyway The Wind Blows' ....Sara Bareilles

'Are You Sitting Comfortably?'.......The Moody Blues

'Beautiful Noise' ....Neil Diamond

'Big Log' ....Robert Plant

'Blowin' In The Wind' ....Bob Dylan

'Both Ends Burning' ....Roxy Music

'Burning Hell'................................Tom Jones

'Candle In The Wind'.....................Elton John

'Don't Force It' ....The Juice

'Don't Stand So Close to Me' ....The Police

'Drop It Like It's Hot' ....Snoop Dogg

'Easy Does It' ....Supertramp

'Four Strong Winds'.......................Neil Young

'Funky Shit' ....The Prodigy

'In The Air Tonight'........................Phil Collins

'I Smell Trouble' ....Buddy Guy

'Let It All Blow'..............................Dazz Band

'Let's Get It Started' ....The Black Eyed Peas

'Push It'..Salt-N-Pepa

'Relax'..Frankie Goes To Hollywood

'Ride Like the Wind' ....Christopher Cross

'Ring of Fire' ....Johnny Cash

'Roll With It'...................................Oasis

'Sit and Wonder'............................The Verve

'Sitting, Waiting, Wishing' ....Jack Johnson

'Something in the Air' ....Thunderclap Newman

'Something's Burning' ....The Stone Roses

'Stuck'...Limp Bizkit

'Stuck In The Middle'....................Mika

'Stuck Like Glue' ....Sugarland

'Stuck On You' ....Lionel Richie

'Taking Care of Business' ....Bachman Turner Overdrive

'The Air That I Breathe'.................The Hollies

'There She Goes'..........................The La's

'The Wind' ....Cat Stevens

'That Smell'...................................Lynyrd Skynyrd

'Waiting For The Miracle'..............Leonard Cohen

'Way Down in the Hole' ....Tom Waits

'We Gotta Get Out Of This Place'..The Animals

'We've Only Just Begun' ....The Carpenters

'Wild Is the Wind'..........................David Bowie

'Wind Beneath My Wings' ....Bette Midler

'Wind of Change'..........................The Scorpions

'Wipe Out'.....................................The Surfaris

'Yellow River' ....Christie

'The littlest room seems to provide the minds of
the Anglo-Saxon race with a greater fund of innocent
amusement than any other single subject.'

DOROTHY L. SAYERS

Did you know?

The Greek philosopher Diogenes thought it was ridiculous to demand privacy when going to the toilet, and thought nothing of relieving himself in the street or marketplace.

Toilet humour 6

If four out of five people suffer from diarrhoea, does that mean that one actually enjoys it?

'You sound like a shit salesman with
a mouthful of samples.'

ANON

Geographic diarrhoea

A popular way of referring to tummy trouble arising from a stay abroad (apart from calling it the squits) is to name it after the city or country where the diarrhoea bug originated, for example:

- Aztec Twostep (applies to anywhere in Mexico)

- Basra Belly (generally applies to anywhere in the Persian Gulf)

- Bombay Belly (even though Bombay is now Mumbai)

- Cairo Craps

- Delhi Belly

- Gringo Gallop (used in Spanish- and Portuguese-speaking countries)

- Gypo/Gyppy Tummy (Egypt)

- Karachi Cork (i.e. what you need to use . . .)

- Montezuma's Revenge (*see* Aztec Twostep)

- Rangoon Runs

- Spanish Tummy

- Tunis Trots

Statistically speaking

British Standards state that the distance from the floor to the top of the toilet seat must be between 405 mm and 435 mm.

Did you know?

According to one of Diana Ross's ex-housekeepers, one of her duties was to flush the soul diva's toilet for her.

To boldly go . . .

Star Trek V: The Final Frontier is the only Star Trek movie to feature a toilet on board the *Enterprise*, along with a sign next to it that reads, 'Do Not Use While In Space Dock'.

As a running joke, bathrooms are never shown in available technical manuals of the *Enterprise*, a gag that started when toilets were accidentally omitted from the original plans. This joke is referenced in the film *Star Trek: First Contact*, in which an exchange includes the line '. . . don't you people from the twenty-fourth century ever pee?'

Potty training

Early passenger trains had no toilets on board. Passengers had to leave the train when it stopped at a station, quickly use the toilets on the platforms, and reboard before their train departed. The first toilets on trains were fitted by the London and North Western Railway in 1850, but only in a special carriage for invalids. It wasn't until the 1880s that toilets appeared regularly on trains in the UK (they were common on US trains about forty years earlier).

NB Some LNWR first-class carriages featured commodes built into the seats.

Grand Theft Toilet

In January 2007, Chelsea and ex-England player Glen Johnson was arrested for attempted toilet seat theft. Johnson, who was on loan to Portsmouth at the time, tried to smuggle the item out of a DIY store in Dartford, Kent with the help of Millwall striker Ben May. Both men were subsequently issued with £80 fixed penalty notices. A store employee who witnessed the theft commented, 'We all recognized Johnson. No one could quite believe a bloke like him, with all that money, would be moronic enough to nick a toilet seat.'

Did you know?

Public toilets in Holland are cleaner thanks to a Dutch company that manufactures urinals with photographs of flies printed on them. They've discovered that men use them for target practice, reducing spillage by up to 80 per cent.

Toilet humour 7

Q: Why are a man's semen white and his urine yellow?

A: So he can tell whether he's coming or going.

Royal toilet deaths

- Edmund II of England died in 1016 allegedly after being stabbed in the bowel while attending the royal outhouse.

- King Wenceslas III of Bohemia was murdered in 1306 with a spear while sitting on the toilet.

- Edward II was killed when a red-hot poker was inserted into his anus while he sat on the toilet at Berkeley Castle in Gloucestershire in 1327.

- In 1760 George II of Great Britain died from an aneurism while sitting on the toilet in Kensington Palace.

- Catherine the Great died of a stroke in 1796 while she was seated on the toilet.

- Emperor Vespasian died on his chamber pot uttering the words, 'Vae, puto deus fio,' meaning, 'Alas, I think I am becoming a god.'

You dirty rat!

In March 2008, fifty-five-year-old Maxine Killingback, who lived alone in Greenwich in south-east London, was attacked by rats that climbed out of her toilet bowl while she was sitting on it. After one rat bit the top of her leg she jumped up and fell on to the floor.

Ms Killingback said, 'It was a big, black one, seven or eight inches long. It was trying to climb up but it kept sliding back down.' She tried flushing the toilet twice but the creature came back each time. Eventually, she drowned the creature by holding it under the water with a plunger. She then barricaded the toilet to stop the other rats that were climbing out.

Greenwich council said she would have to wait three weeks for them to come and deal with the problem, during which time Maxine decided to leave her apartment and stay with a friend. She said, 'You don't expect to sit down to spend a penny and be bitten by a rat.'

Toilet humour 8

Old Aunt Gladys went to her doctor to see what could be done about her constipation.

'It's terrible,' she told him, 'I haven't moved my bowels in a week.'

'I see,' said the doctor. 'Have you done anything about it?' he asked.

'Of course I have,' she replied, 'I sit on the toilet for an hour in the morning and another hour at night.'

'That's not what I mean,' the doctor said, 'Do you take anything?'

'Naturally,' she answered. 'I take a large book.'

The writing's on the stall!

A selection of some creative toilet graffiti:

- In a music college: 'You need to wiggle the Handel.' Underneath someone had written, 'If I do, will it wiggle Bach?'

- 'Everybody pisses on the floor. Be a hero and shit on the ceiling.'

- Above a urinal: 'Don't look here for humour. The joke's in your hand.'

- 'Don't beam me up Scotty, I'm in the middle of a sh . . .'

- 'Don't throw your cigarette butts in the urinal. It makes them soggy and hard to light. Thank you. The Janitor.'

- 'Love is blind. God is love. Stevie Wonder is blind therefore Stevie Wonder is God.'

- Written at the very bottom of a dividing partition: 'Beware of limbo dancers!'

- 'A pill in time saves nine months.'

- 'If at first you don't succeed, you're average.'

- 'I smell sh*t. Is there an estate agent in here?'

- 'I tried to drown my troubles but my husband learned to swim.'

- 'I'm not prejudiced. I hate everyone.'

- 'The difference between genius and stupidity is that genius has its limits.'

- 'You must walk backwards 'cos all I see is an asshole.'

- 'Look out for No.1. Don't step in No. 2.'

- 'Boycott shampoo! Demand the real poo!'

Did you know?

That story about Sir Walter Raleigh placing his cloak on the ground so that Queen Elizabeth I could avoid stepping on a puddle is only half true. Given the sanitary conditions of the time it was more likely to have been a puddle of urine rather than water.

Analyse this!

Dr Gilda Carle, a renowned psychotherapist and consultant for toilet paper manufacturer Cottonelle, has this to say about which way the toilet paper is orientated in your bathroom:

If the top sheet is rolled over, you crave organization, like taking charge and are likely to over-achieve.

If the top sheet is rolled under, you're laid-back, dependable and seek relationships with strong foundations.

If you don't care as long as the paper's there, you aim to minimize conflict, value flexibility and like putting yourself in new situations.

Did you know?

The opposite of defecation is micturition, the act of urinating.

Toilet humour 9

It is a young man's first day as a waiter at a truck-stop diner. A large trucker sits down at the counter and places his order. 'Give me three flat tyres and a couple of headlights.'

The young man looks confused but writes this down and tells the cook. 'I think he's in the wrong place. Look what he wants to eat.'

The cook shakes his head. 'It's slang. Three flat tyres and a couple of headlights means he wants three pancakes and two eggs sunny-side up'.

'Oh,' says the young man, but then takes the trucker a bowl of baked beans.

'What the hell's this?' says the trucker. 'I didn't order this!'

'No you didn't,' the waiter says. 'But while you're waiting for your parts I thought you might as well gas up.'

Straight to Number One

Known as the 'Elton John of Mozambique', forty-four-year-old Feliciano dos Santos is a rock star who sings about topics with a difference: toilets and clean water. Born in a poor village in the province of Niassa, Feliciano's mission to spread the word about hygiene was driven in part by the fact he was disabled as child by polio, a disease spread by bad sanitation.

Feliciano and his band take songs with public health messages around Mozambique villages. One of his most popular is 'Wash Your Hands'.

❖ ❖ ❖ ❖ ❖ ❖ ❖ ❖ ❖ ❖ ❖ ❖ ❖ ❖ ❖ ❖

Toilet humour 10

Did you hear about the constipated accountant?
He couldn't budget.

Did you hear about the constipated composer?
He couldn't finish the last movement.

Did you hear about the constipated mathematician?
He worked it out with a pencil.

❖ ❖ ❖ ❖ ❖ ❖ ❖ ❖ ❖ ❖ ❖ ❖ ❖ ❖ ❖ ❖

That's just gross!

At some weddings in North Africa, the bride's urine is sprinkled on the guests as part of the ceremony.

This invention could save your marriage!

In 1996, to get round the age-old problem of different preferences for hanging toilet rolls, a Dallas-based industrial engineer Curtis Batts invented the Tilt-A-Roll, a swivelling toilet-paper dispenser. As its name suggests, this allows the holder to be rotated 180 degrees so that the toilet paper can be unrolled from over or under the roll as desired. The inspiration for Batts's invention derives from his parents' constant bickering over toilet paper placement – a practice also shared by him and his wife. The device's motto is 'Let Tilt-A-Roll save your marriage!'

Potty promotion

In the US a Midwest plumbing company used the slogan, 'We're Number One in a Number Two Business'.

Did you know?

Many Victorian children roamed the London streets collecting dog mess, selling it to tanners for use in tanning leather (the enzymes it contained helped preserve the skins).

Creepers and Sneakers:
20 types of fart

1 **Baritone Bowl Blow**: any fart that resonates around the toilet bowl with a deep, satisfying echo.

2 **Big Chief Howling Wind**: any fart that's so raucous that there's a two-second delay before anyone can pass comment.

3 **Bachelor**: extra loud fart of long duration, often signifying the farter lives on their own.

4 **Bubble Maker**: any underwater fart.

5 **Bun Buster**: a fart that delivers pain and noise in equal measure and which threatens not only to rip the seams of your trousers, but possibly your rectum too.

6 **Crop Duster**: a series of long farts emitted while walking briskly.

7 **Cushion Creeper**: a muffled fart that never seems to end, half absorbed into the fabric of a cushion or well-padded chair or sofa.

8 **Dutch Oven**: any fart made in bed and held captive by the covers. Good for hastening the end of a relationship.

9 **Freedom Fart**: high-pitched fart, usually a result of it not being restrained by any form of clothing or seating.

10 **Gambler**: a fart on the verge of something far more solid.

11 **Lift Painter**: any fart issued in a confined space.

12 **Mersey Cheer**: disappointing, spluttering fart, like the intermittent applause heard at a Liverpool FC home game.

13 **One Cheek Sneak**: the art of surreptitiously lifting one buttock to let a fart secretly escape.

14 **Poopie Prologue**: a fart that is followed mere seconds later by a number two.

15 **Running Multi-Fart**: a favourite among children playing; the closest you can get to making music with your rectum.

16 **SBD**: abbreviation for Silent But Deadly. No noise but plenty of stink.

17 **Squeaker**: quiet and unsatisfying. Hardly worth the trouble, really.

18 **Toad Stepper**: short, sharp, fart that replicates the sound a toad would make if trodden on.

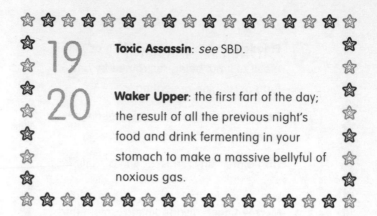

19   **Toxic Assassin**: *see* SBD.

20   **Waker Upper**: the first fart of the day; the result of all the previous night's food and drink fermenting in your stomach to make a massive bellyful of noxious gas.

Statistically speaking

Humans produce roughly 500 litres of urine and 50 litres of faeces per person per year.

Did you know?

If a girl wanted to end a relationship in seventeenth-century Germany, she didn't need to worry about the whole 'it isn't you, it's me' thing. All she needed to do was put a small piece of her excrement in her unwanted lover's shoe.

Toilet humour 11

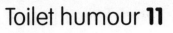

Four farmers were sitting in the village pub. At the table next to them sat a young girl reading a book.

The first farmer said, 'I think it's WOOOMB.'

The second replied, 'No, it must be WOOOOOOOOMBHHH.'

The third said, 'That's rubbish. It has to be WOOM.'

The fourth farmer says, 'You're all wrong! It's WOOMMMMMMMMMBBB.'

Hearing this, the young lady could stand it no longer. She put her book down and leaned over to the farmers saying, 'Look. It's WOMB spelt W.O.M.B. That's it. There are no variations, no alternatives! There's no argument about it!' Exasperated, she left the pub.

Eventually, one of the stunned farmers broke the silence by saying, 'Did you hear that? A mere slip of a girl and a townie too. How on earth would she know what a prize bull's fart sounds like?'

'Wherefore my bowels should sound like a harp.'

ISAIAH 16:11

Odd Toilet Laws

1 In Switzerland, a man may not relieve himself while standing up after 10 p.m.

2 In Scotland if someone knocks on your door and requests the use of your toilet, you must allow them access.

3 In the UK a pregnant woman may relieve herself anywhere she likes, including (if she requests) in a policeman's helmet.

4 In Dana Point, California, it's illegal to open the window when you are using the bathroom.

5 In Indonesia it is against the law to leave a public toilet without flushing it.

6 In Britain a man may legally urinate in public, but only if it is on the rear wheel of his motor vehicle and his right hand remains on the vehicle.

7 On Waldron Island, Washington State, it's illegal to have more than two toilets in a house. (This law was introduced to conserve water but people are going to use the toilet as many times as they want, regardless of the number of toilets!)

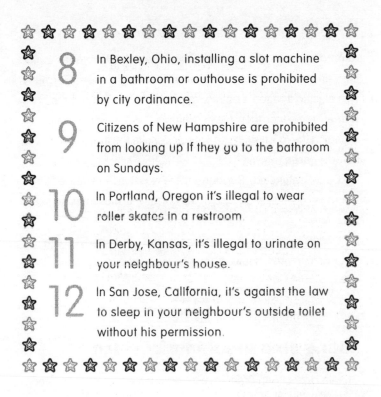

8 In Bexley, Ohio, installing a slot machine in a bathroom or outhouse is prohibited by city ordinance.

9 Citizens of New Hampshire are prohibited from looking up if they go to the bathroom on Sundays.

10 In Portland, Oregon it's illegal to wear roller skates in a restroom.

11 In Derby, Kansas, it's illegal to urinate on your neighbour's house.

12 In San Jose, California, it's against the law to sleep in your neighbour's outside toilet without his permission.

Did you know?

Prince Charles is said to take his own white leather toilet seat with him wherever he travels.

Dennis Bueller's Day Off

According to a report in the *Daily Mirror* in November 2008, thirteen-year-old Dennis Bueller of Recklinghausen, Germany was blasted through a bathroom window after spraying the bowl with air freshener then playing around with a lighter while still sitting on the toilet. With predictable results the flame ignited the aerosol gases.

Dennis later said, 'Suddenly there was this big orange flame. I woke up outside with my clothes burned off me, smelling like a barbecue.'

Dennis suffered burns to his face and upper body. His father Artur commented, 'He realizes he was a bit dim.'

Sitting on a great musical idea

Charlie Deal of San Francisco found another more creative and profitable use for toilet seats: transforming them into electric guitars. Each Deal Guitar was as unique as the toilet seat from which it was handmade. And, according to those who played the instruments, they were far from a novelty: their construction and finish were first-rate, and the sound reproduction was exceptional.

The Deal Guitar Business was founded in 1968 and guitars were played by some of the biggest names of the era, including Jefferson Airplane and Starship. The cover of Huey Lewis's platinum-selling album *Sports* prominently features a Charlie Deal toilet-seat guitar.

Toilet humour **12**

After going shopping at lunchtime a woman gets into the lift at work. Just as the doors close she feels a particularly large fart coming on. As there's no one in the lift she lets rip but it stinks. Looking in her bag she finds a can of air freshener that she's just bought and she sprays it all around her. She just manages to put it back in her bag when the door opens at the next floor and a man gets in. He sniffs the air and looks uncomfortable.

'Is there something wrong?' asks the woman.

'Sure,' says the man. 'It's the smell in here.'

'I noticed that too,' she says. 'Do you think it's air freshener?'

'Hell, no!' he says. 'It smells like someone took a shit in a pine tree.'

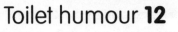

Dr Charles Gerba, an American microbiologist, claims that the bathroom is actually cleaner than the kitchen, and that as far as bacteria are concerned, it's safer to make a sandwich on the top of a toilet bowl than the work surface.

Wiping out inflation

During Zimbabwe's hyperinflation of 2008 (230 million per cent) it was cheaper to use money as toilet paper than actual toilet paper. The maths is simple; a roll of toilet paper contains 350 sheets and at that time cost about $1.50. That meant that each sheet was worth $0.004 or the equivalent of 3,600 Zimbabwe dollars. Using a 1,000-Zimbabwe-dollar note to wipe yourself made sound financial sense.

Leading Lavatories

Who knew the WC played such a significant role in cinema? Here is a selection of the greatest toilet appearances:

- *Back to the Future* (1985): Doc Brown comes up with the idea of the Flux Capacitor (which makes time travel possible) after slipping off the toilet and banging his head.

- *Lethal Weapon 2* (1989): Danny Glover's character finds himself sitting on a toilet that's booby-trapped to explode as soon as he gets up from it.

- *Home Alone 2* (1992): Joe Pesci gets his head set on fire and then attempts to put it out by sticking it down a toilet bowl which, unknown to him, is filled with kerosene.

- *Blown Away* (1994): Tommy Lee Jones uses a toilet bowl in his prison cell to make a home-made bomb that blows a hole in the prison wall.

- *Jurassic Park* (1993): A lawyer is eaten by a Tyrannosaurus Rex while hiding in an outhouse.

- *Pulp Fiction* (1994): John Travolta is shot by Bruce Willis as he's leaving a bathroom; he falls back on to the toilet, dead.

- *Meet the Fockers* (2004): Robert De Niro's cat Jinxie flushes the Fockers' dog down the toilet.

- *Arachnophobia* (1990): A large spider hides on the inside of the toilet bowl just waiting for someone to use it . . .

- *Trainspotting* (1996): Ewan McGregor is fishing around in a toilet bowl to find his opium suppositories, eventually plunging in and emerging in a beautiful coral reef.

- *The Godfather* (1972): To kill a rival and a crooked cop, Al Pacino (Michael) retrieves a planted gun that has been hidden behind a restaurant toilet.

- *The Naked Gun* (1998): Lieutenant Frank Drebbin (Lesley Nielsen) goes for a toilet break in the middle of a press conference still fully miked-up. The result is the public transmission of the sound of relentless urination.

- *There's Something About Mary* (1998): Ben Stiller gets his manhood caught in his zipper just before his prom date with Cameron Diaz.

- *Dumb and Dumber* (1994): After drinking Turbo-Lax and finding that he's blocked the toilet, Jeff Daniels rips it off its fixtures and empties the entire contents out of a window.

- *GoldenEye* (1995): James Bond kills a Russian soldier on the toilet after uttering the witticism, 'Beg your pardon. I forgot to knock'.

- *Snakes on a Plane* (2006): A character is bitten on the penis by a snake hiding inside an aircraft toilet.

- *Fight Club* (1999): Tyler Durden (Brad Pitt) and his mob corner a city official in a toilet cubicle and threaten to cut his testicles off.

- *Hostel* (2005): The Dutch businessman is attacked in a toilet cubicle. Two of his fingers are cut off and then he's almost drowned before being knifed to death.

- *2001, A Space Odyssey* (1968): features a zero-gravity toilet, complete with comprehensive instructions for use.

- *The Way We Were* (1973): Robert Redford vomits violently into Barbra Streisand's toilet and, in the next scene, makes love to her.

- *Candyman* (1992): the eponymous hook-handed killer appears after his name is said three times while looking in a bathroom mirror.

- *Terminator 3* (2003): T-X and Arnie destroy a whole row of toilet cubicles as they knock the hell out of each other in a bathroom.

- *The Pink Panther Strikes Again* (1976): two assassins get into bathroom stalls on either side of Inspector Clouseau. He drops the toilet paper, reaches down to get it, and the assassins shoot each other.

And of course . . .

- *Carry On at Your Convenience* (1971): a tale of industrial strife at the lavatory factory of W.C. Boggs, played by Kenneth Williams.

Toilet humour 13

There was a Native American named Chief Bowels who was very angry. The town wanted to build a new golf course on his reservation and he decided to protest.

He sent one of his men to deliver a note to the council office. Unfortunately, there was a medical centre in the same building and the messenger entered the wrong door. He handed a doctor the note that said 'Bowels not move!' The doctor gave the man a pill to take back to the Chief.

The next day, the Chief's messenger returned and handed the doctor another note that said 'Bowels still not move!' This time the doctor gave him a stronger pill.

The next day the same thing happened. The messenger delivered another letter that read 'Bowels STILL not move!' This time the doctor handed him the strongest pill he had.

The following day the messenger came back with a note that said, 'You win. Bowels HAD to move! Teepee full of shit!'

That's just gross!

Following a trip to Mecca in the 1850s, the explorer Sir Richard Burton reported on the Muslim practice of wiping the penis on stone, sand or a clod of earth after urination. He observed men carrying these materials under their turbans for this purpose.

First paper, then toilet paper

Ts'ai Lun, a Chinese court official, is believed to have invented paper in AD 105. It only took a short leap of imagination to develop this new material into toilet paper – an act that was viewed with suspicion by many travellers (in AD 851 a Muslim merchant commented that wiping with paper instead of cleaning with his hand and water, which he was used to, was a 'foul habit').

By AD 1391, toilet paper was in common use and the Chinese Bureau of Imperial Supplies recorded a production level of 720,000 sheets each year just for the Imperial Court, with the Imperial Family itself enjoying specially prepared soft, perfumed paper.

'Dear Sir, I am in the smallest room of the house. I have your letter before me. Soon it will be behind me.'

WINSTON CHURCHILL, REPLYING TO AN UNWELCOME LETTER

Toilet humour 14

A girl invites her boyfriend to meet her parents. He's very nervous about making a good impression and by the time he reaches her house his stomach is in turmoil, gurgling and burbling.

Although still very anxious, he is actually getting on quite well with what could turn out to be his future in-laws but, halfway though dinner, he realizes his previous nervousness is going to cause him to fart. He holds it in as long as possible but eventually the pain and pressure are too much and he lets rip.

'Spot!' shouts out his girlfriend's mother to the family dog, who is lying at the young man's feet.

The boy is so relieved that the dog got the blame and decides to let another fart go, this one louder.

'Spot!' the mother shouts out sharply.

'I'm home and dry!' the boy thinks and, this time, lets loose the loudest fart yet.

'Spot!!!' shrieks the mother. 'Get over here before he shits on you!'

Statistically speaking

Most people fart between ten and twenty times a day.
The quantity of gas expelled would be enough to inflate
a small balloon.

Famous Farters

- The Roman Emperor Claudius decreed that 'all Roman citizens shall be allowed to pass gas whenever necessary'. (Unfortunately Emperor Constantine later reversed this decision in a 315 BC edict.)

- The diarist Samuel Pepys commented, 'Wind doth now and then torment me about the fundament extremely.'

- Queen Victoria ate too quickly and mixed claret with malt whisky. As a result she suffered from persistent flatulence.

- Adolf Hitler's personal physician, Theodore Morrell, used to prescribe regular 'anti-gas' medication for the Führer. His flatulence is thought to be a result of his fondness for Bavarian sausage and game pie, even though he was widely believed to have been a vegetarian. Pills the Führer took for his condition contained strychnine and belladonna, which are known for causing hallucinations and violent behaviour.

- Salvador Dalí was a prolific farter who was said to be able to extinguish a candle from a distance of 6 feet.

The Eight Unwritten Laws of
Male Restroom Etiquette

1. URINALS ARE ONLY FOR URINATION

If you need to freshen up, use the washbasin. If you need to do a number two, use a cubicle. In polite society there are absolutely no exceptions to this rule.

2. USE THE SPACE

Men should be distributed as widely as possible among the available urinals. Where practical, choose a urinal with a free space each side. Where this isn't possible and you have a urinal neighbour, ensure you follow rules 3, 4 and 5.

3. NO TALKING

If you want to make new friends do it at school, college, work, the gym, the PTA, the golf course, the football match or even online . . . anywhere but the toilet. A trip to the men's room should be considered a solitary experience, not an opportunity to engage anyone else in conversation and especially not a chance to ask them out for a drink.

4. FACE THE FRONT

Count the tiles, study the grouting, check the form that states when the bathroom was last cleaned or even read an irrelevant advertisement – boring but a necessary part of restroom etiquette. Unless you want your neighbour to think you're sizing him up do not, under any circumstances, turn your head even a few degrees to the left or right.

5. AVOID THE BLIND SPOT

If standing next to a neighbour, ensure you remain in his peripheral vision. Standing too far back puts you in his blind spot where the natural inclination is for you to be perceived as a killer or a sexual predator. Or both.

6. AIM TRUE

It should go without saying but the target for your urine should be the drain hole or the coloured deodorizing 'mint' at the base of the urinal. No one is asking for Robin Hood-style accuracy but it's not that difficult at point-blank range to avoid the restroom wall, the floor, your shoes or, more importantly, your neighbour's shoes.

7. CHECK FOR FEET

Never assume that a bathroom stall that appears open is unoccupied – the door might be broken or the occupant might have genuinely forgotten to lock it. A quick foot check will avoid embarrassment. When you do push the door, do it slowly. If there is an occupant this will give him time to stop shooting up, having one off the wrist or to cover his embarrassment while shouting, 'Hey buddy!'

8. TURDS AREN'T FOR SHARING

Dropping a turd in the bowl is not the same as becoming a father (in fact there are many differences). This means you don't have to share your new creation with everyone. Flush until all trace of your last meal has disappeared from view. If you're beaming with pride and really feel like sharing your joy with someone, take a photo of it and show your co-workers, family or friends. Then again, don't.

Did you know?

In the Apache and Mojave Indian tribes men used to urinate squatting down while the women did it standing up.

Toilet humour 15

Two men were playing golf when the first one said, 'I really need to take a dump.'

The second guy replied, 'Well there's a large tree by the next green. Go behind it and do your stuff.'

The first man looks over at the tree and remarks, 'But I don't have any toilet paper.'

Being resourceful, his friend says, 'You have a dollar on you don't you? It's an emergency so use that to wipe yourself.'

Reluctantly, the first guy goes and does his business. Minutes later he comes back with crap all over his hands.

His friend asks, 'What the hell happened? Didn't you use the dollar like I said?'

'Sure, but have you ever tried to wipe your ass with three quarters, two dimes, and a nickel?'

Death by toilet paper

The Nigerian *Sunday Sun* newspaper reported on an ingenious assassination plot that took place in 2006. A man's enemies discovered that their victim suffered from bad haemorrhoids. After finding out what toilet paper his wife bought, they purchased the same brand and coated the paper with a deadly toxin. Gaining access to his house, they substituted their own roll and waited for results.

Sure enough, in wiping himself, the poison entered his bloodstream via his piles, resulting in his death from a heart attack.

What type of farter are you?

AMBITIOUS: Constantly attempts to beat his own record for loudness, duration or smell.

ANTISOCIAL: Farts immediately after the lift doors close.

ARROGANT: Thinks everyone else absolutely, positively wants to hear his farts.

ATHLETIC: Farts while performing a cartwheel or a back flip.

BEWILDERED: Not sure if the fart is his or not.

CARELESS: Farts in church or at a solemn funeral service.

CAVALIER: Farts anywhere, any place, anyhow.

CHILDISH: Farts and then giggles.

CHIVALROUS: Leaves the room to fart if there are ladies present.

CONCEITED: Thinks he can out-fart anyone.

CONFUSED: Never sure whether to fart or belch. Sometimes does neither. Sometimes both.

CONSIDERATE: Only farts in the bathroom.

DISAPPOINTED: Produces silent farts.

DISHONEST: Farts and then blames the dog.

EGOTIST: Farts without anyone else present, solely for his own pleasure.

ENVIRONMENTALIST: Farts regularly but feels guilty about global warming.

EXHIBITIONIST: Lights his own farts to create a spectacular indoor firework display.

GIFTED: Smells your farts and can tell what you've been eating.

IMPUDENT: Farts out aloud and then laughs.

MASOCHIST: Farts in bed then pulls the covers over himself.

MISERABLE: Really feels like farting, but can't.

MUSICAL: Farts over a three-octave range.

NOSTALGIC: Thinks that farting sure ain't what it used to be.

PHILOSOPHER: 'I fart, therefore I am.'

POSH: Calls farting 'flatulence' or 'breaking wind'.

PREMATURE: Farts suddenly without any long, satisfying build-up.

PRUDENT: Always has farts in reserve.

RECKLESS: Farts near the presence of a naked flame.

SADIST: Farts in bed then pulls the covers over his wife or girlfriend.

SCIENTIFIC: Bottles his farts so he can analyse the gas composition.

SENSITIVE: Farts and then starts crying, blaming a childhood incident for his flatulence.

SENTIMENTAL: Thinks about previous farts with a small tear in his eye.

SLOB: Farts violently, stains his pants and wears the same underwear for seventy-two hours.

SNOB: Will only fart à la carte.

SOCIABLE: Likes the smell of other people's farts.

STRATEGIC: Farts but disguises it with loud, simultaneous coughing.

SUBSERVIENT: Asks for permission to fart.

THESPIAN: Farts and pauses dramatically for applause.

THRIFTY: Farts when he's cold.

TIMID: Is startled by his own farts.

UNFORTUNATE: Farts but leaves something solid in his pants.

VAIN: Loves the smell of his own farts.

Toilet humour 16

A drunk gets up from the bar and walks into the gents. A few minutes later, a high-pitched blood-curdling cry can be heard. Two minutes later there's the same scream and the same thing happens two minutes after that.

One of the barmen goes into the toilet to investigate what's going on. He shouts at the only locked toilet door.

'Are you in there?'

The drunk answers, 'Yes.'

'Well what's all the screaming about? You're scaring my customers!'

The drunk replies, 'I've just had a shit and every time I try to flush, something comes up and squeezes the hell out of my balls. See for yourself.'

The drunk unlocks the door and the barman looks in and says, 'You bloody fool! You're sitting on the mop bucket!'

Statistically speaking

About a third of all Americans flush the toilet while they're still sitting on it.

Feng shui and bathrooms

According to proponents of feng shui, the location of the bathroom in your house can impact your health, your wealth, your love life and even harmony within your family. Follow these authentic tips to prevent chi (the natural energy of the universe) from flowing out of your house:

- Locations which can have negative effect on your well-being include bathrooms above the front door or the kitchen and bathrooms under the stairs.

- A bathroom in the hallway, close to the door, can drain chi away before it has a chance to circulate through the rest of the home.

- The worst place, however, is a bathroom in the centre of a home. According to feng shui, a centrally located bathroom can destabilize the energy of the entire home.

- A bathroom should not be directly parallel to your bedroom in any way, i.e. above, below or opposite it, since you might absorb negative energy while you are sleeping.

- If your bathroom is in the 'wrong' location you can reduce or stabilize any negative chi by placing 'earth-type' objects such as a bowl of pebbles, a large crystal or a fresh flower arrangement on the toilet tank or on a shelf above the toilet. Alternatively, they can be placed in the corners of the room.

- Other remedies include painting the walls red, placing a red or black floor mat at the base of the washbasin and hanging a mirror on the outside of the door. Gold-coloured towels are also recommended.

- It's good to place bamboo plants in the bathroom, especially where they can be reflected in a mirror.

- Tie a red ribbon or wind red tape around all outgoing water pipes.

- Always replace the toilet lid and close the bathroom door to prevent the unnecessary escape of chi.

- Ensure that the toilet and the bathtub have space between them; if they are too close the chi will not flow as it should.

- Everything should be in good working order and clean to promote good feng shui. Dirty or broken items in the bathroom will accentuate negative energy.

Did you know?

In the fifteenth century the cardinals of Rome needed somewhere very private for their discussions that would eventually lead to the selection of Pope Pius II. They met in a toilet . . .

'Stick with me kid and you'll be farting through silk.'
ROBERT MITCHUM, TO HIS FUTURE WIFE.

Fart definitions

DISCOMFART: The feeling one gets when trying to hold in particularly intense flatulence.

FARTALISM: The sense of inevitability when you realize you can't hold it in any longer.

FARTALITY: Death following acute, prolonged and explosive farting.

FARTASTIC: Descriptive of a hugely satisfying, echoing fart.

FARTASY: A whimsical fart.

FART-FORWARD: The act of expelling farts as quickly as possible in the hope that no one will really notice.

FARTIGUE: Exhaustion arising from an excess of farting.

FART MAJEURE: A fart of hurricane-like proportions.

FART PAS: Any fart perceived as a real social blunder.

FART-PROOFING: Using strong aftershave or perfume to cloak a particularly noxious smell.

FARTUNATE: Finding yourself in the fortuitous position of farting in public and no one noticing.

MISFARTUNE: The bad luck associated with a discreet fart resulting in something far more solid.

PIANOFARTE: A melodious fart that begins quietly and ends in a strident crescendo.

Did you know?

It's claimed that to ensure your hands are germ-free after using the toilet, you should wash them long enough to sing 'Twinkle, Twinkle, Little Star' all the way through.

Toilet humour 17

Did you hear about Robin Hood's very small house?

It has a little John.

The Royal Wee

Queen Victoria was so shocked and saddened by the death of her beloved Prince Albert from typhoid in 1861 that she ordered that no changes be made to their living accommodation at Windsor Castle, effectively freezing it in time. Unfortunately this decree meant that none of the fifty-three cesspits at the Castle could be emptied, leading to their overflowing and the subsequent death of a number of royal servants from disease.

That's just gross!

➡ **A Zimbabwe aphrodisiac is made from baboon urine mixed with beer.**

Logging on ...

For those who pass the time in the toilet playing with their phone comes iPoo, an iPhone application that, according to the developers, 'brings together pooers from around the world'. When you open iPoo you're instantly connected with other iPoo users who are also taking a dump. You can write messages or make drawings on a virtual bathroom wall that are visible to other iPoo users. You can even see where they're sitting using the application's map view!

The bottom of the social order

Under the Hindu caste system in India, servants will clean any part of a house except the latrines. This privilege is left for the lowest of the low, the Untouchables. Considered too impure to rank as worthy beings, these outcasts are equipped with nothing more sophisticated than a brush and bucket or pieces of cardboard and have to carry away the waste in baskets placed on their heads for minimal payment – usually less than £1 a month.

did you know?

So she didn't have to leave the banquet, when Anne Boleyn married Henry VIII two handmaidens were hidden under the table, one to hold the pot and the other with a lace handkerchief.

Toilet humour **18**

Q: How many men does it take to change a roll of toilet paper?

A: I don't know – it's never happened.

Taking the piss

In alternative medicine, the term 'urine therapy' refers to the practice of using one's own urine for medicinal or cosmetic purposes, a custom adopted by some of the earliest civilizations and still common in some circles today.

- In Roman times, there was a tradition among the Gauls to use their urine to whiten teeth (the ammonia within it acted as a bleach).

- The Roman scholar and philosopher Pliny believed that peeing on his own feet each morning contributed to his general well-being.

- The ancient Greek historian Herodutus believed that the urine of 'newly deflowered' girls was ideal for curing eye-related illnesses.

- Inuits used urine to clean their hair while Mexicans recommended it as a great cure for dandruff.

- In China, the urine of young boys has been regarded as having medicinal qualities.

- The Aztecs used urine to sterilize and heal wounds, a practice still followed by Saharan Bedouins and some Alaskan Inuits.

- In parts of southern China, babies' faces are washed with urine to protect the skin.

- The French used to soak stockings in urine and wrap them around their necks in order to cure the contagious disease strep throat.

- Aristocratic French women in the seventeenth century were reported to have bathed in urine to beautify their skin.

- In England during the 1860s and 1870s, drinking urine was a common cure for jaundice.

- The extended ages reached by Tibetan yogis and lamas are said to be the result of drinking their own urine.

- In Sierra Madre, Mexico, farmers would prepare poultices for broken bones by using a mixture of urine and powdered charred corn. This was made into a paste and applied to the skin.

- In the thirteenth century, Pope John XXI recommended urine as effective eyewash.

- Applying fresh urine to the face with a small towel or flannel early in the day, allowing it to dry, and then washing it off has been known to reduce acne in some people.

- Sportsmen and dancers claim that urinating on their own feet can prevent athlete's foot or even cure it. Madonna admitted on *The David Letterman Show* to adopting this practice.

- Some people urinate on the hands or feet to soften calluses. Dolores O'Riordan, from Irish band The Cranberries, admitted that when she was learning to play the guitar she had a problem with calluses on her fingers which urine therapy alleviated.

- In the last stages of cancer, Steve McQueen is said to have survived solely on a diet of urine and boiled alligator skin prescribed by his Mexican doctors.

- Jim Morrison and John Lennon are both said to have experimented with urine therapy.

- Rubbing a mixture of potato, sulphur powder and heated, old urine into the scalp is said to help reduce hair loss.

- One of the most famous proponents of urine therapy was Morarji Desai, the Prime Minister of India from 1977 to 1979. On the occasion of his ninety-ninth birthday in 1995, Desai attributed his longevity to drinking his morning urine on a daily basis.

- Mahatma Gandhi is said to have drunk his own urine in the belief that it purified his soul.

Did you know?

It's not the actual colour of the urine per se that gives an indication as to your health, but the intensity of that colour. Health experts say that you should 'pee pale'. If urine is dark then it indicates you're not drinking enough water.

Wake up and smell the coffee

In 1994, workers at the Wire Rope Corporation of America in St Joseph, Missouri were puzzled as to why their morning coffee had tasted particularly foul over a number of weeks, so they set up a hidden video camera to monitor their kitchen area. After viewing tapes from the first day's filming they found the reason: their co-worker, forty-one-year-old Milton Ross, had been filmed urinating into the coffee pot.

Ross was immediately fired and was later charged with assault. Local health investigators stated that they didn't believe that any communicable diseases had been contracted by drinking the spiked coffee.

Statistically speaking

According to a survey conducted by the University of Arizona, a lift button is host to forty times more bacteria than a public toilet seat.

Toilet humour 19

A Sunday school teacher was concerned that his infant class might be confused by the commercialism of Christmas and wanted to make sure that they understood that the birth of the Lord really took place. He asked his class, 'Where is Jesus today?'

Michael raised his hand and said, 'He's in heaven.'

Louise raised her hand and answered, 'He's in my heart.'

Little Johnny, who was waving his hand furiously in the air shouted out, 'I know, I know! He's in our bathroom!'

The rest of the class looked confused and the teacher frowned. Eventually he asked Little Johnny how he knew that the Son of God was in his bathroom.

Little Johnny said, 'Well, every morning, my father gets up, bangs on the bathroom door and yells, "Jesus Christ, are you still in there?"'

Did you know?

In case of an accident the door of a Superloo (or to give it its proper title, Automatic Public Convenience), is programmed to open automatically after fifteen minutes.

Oh ... it's you again!

In a scene that could have come straight out of *Blackadder*, Edward de Vere, a prominent court official in the reign of Queen Elizabeth I, accidentally passed wind while bowing to Her Majesty. So embarrassed was he by this accident that he decided to leave the country. After seven years of travelling abroad he decided to return to the court whereupon he presented himself once more to the Queen. Elizabeth was very surprised to see him and was supposed to have remarked, 'My lord. I had forgotten the wind.'

That's just gross!

One gram of faeces can contain 10 million viruses, 1 million bacteria, one thousand parasite cysts and one hundred parasite eggs.

Letting it all out

The danger of stifling farts has long been recognized. To ensure his citizens didn't suffer stomach cramps or constipation, Emperor Claudius I passed a law permitting people to break wind freely in public. And, in the fifteenth to sixteenth centuries, the classical scholar Erasmus wrote a treatise all about flatulence, in which he warned that a stifled fart (he didn't use those exact words) was a serious health hazard.

According to the famous German physician Carl Ludwig, most nineteenth-century women suffered from chronic constipation – so terrified were they of farting after dinner that they continually clenched their buttocks.

You're out of order!

In September 1965, the Rolling Stones were travelling through London's East End in a chauffeur-driven Daimler when Bill Wyman desperately needed to relieve himself. Their driver pulled into a petrol station and Wyman rushed out, only to find that the toilet was out of order.

Not having any of this, Wyman went back to the car and told Mick Jagger, who, along with Brian Jones, started arguing with the manager, telling him, 'We piss anywhere, man!' Three of the four Rolling Stones then urinated against the forecourt wall.

Police were called and the band members were arrested. In court they were described as 'shaggy-haired monsters' and were each fined £3 for 'insulting behaviour'.

Toilet humour 20

Two blondes and a brunette are walking down a street when a bird shits on one of the blondes.

The brunette says to her friends, 'Stay here. I'll go and get some toilet paper.'

Just after she leaves, one blonde turns to the other and says, 'How stupid is she? By the time she gets back, that bird will be miles away.'

All part of the job

One of the problems that comes with being the size of a sumo wrestler (average weight 23 stone) is that you're too large to reach around and wipe your own bottom . . . which is why novice wrestlers are used for this unpleasant but necessary task. Given this duty it's no surprise to learn that six out of ten novices quit within one year of their sumo apprenticeship.

Did you know?

King Henry II had a court jester called Roland who would entertain guests at royal banquets by farting (life was so much simpler then).

Caught short

When Portuguese explorer Ferdinand Magellan's fleet of five sailing boats set out to circumnavigate the globe in 1519, each ship carried 'fifty casks of water, fresh and pure'. His crew members knew that they'd have to locate water along the way; however, after eighteen months and in uncharterod waters, there was no source of fresh water to be found. The only alternative was to drink their own urine. One crewman wrote in his journal, 'It was surprisingly not unsavoury, having no worse a taste than a flagon most foul with rancid port, as many I have tasted before.'

Caught offside

The Spanish First Division footballer David Billabone was playing for his club Bilbao against Cadiz when he was suddenly caught short. Unable to wait until half-time, Billabone decided to urinate discretely behind his team's goalposts, forgetting that it's hard to be discreet in front of twenty thousand fans and photographers. The resulting photograph appeared all over the Spanish press and Billabone was fined the equivalent of £2,000.

Rhubarb, rhubarb . . .

The eighteenth-century Chinese Emperor Qianlong planned to conquer Europe without firing a shot. His cunning scheme was to ban the export of rhubarb from China, resulting in, he assumed, mass constipation across the whole of Europe and a willingness to surrender.

Did you know?

The Chicago Pizza Pie Factory in Hanover Square, London had very creative names for its toilet doors. The gents' were labelled 'Elton John' and the ladies' Olivia Newton John'.

Toilet humour 21

An elderly lady goes to her GP complaining about her flatulence, telling him that although she farts many times each day, it's more of a nuisance than a real problem.

'What do you mean?' asks her doctor.

'Well,' says the old lady, 'They're silent and they don't smell.'

The doctor writes a prescription and tells her to come back in a week.

When she returns she says, 'I don't know what you gave me doctor! I still fart all day and although they're still silent, they now stink the place up!'

The doctor nods and says, 'Now that we've cleared up your sinuses, I'll see what I can do about your hearing.'

Crap cartoons

South Park's Mr Hankey was not TV's first talking turd character. That honour goes to Dr Shit, a popular (if not subtle) character on the Japanese programme *Ugo Ugo Ruga*.

If you think that's odd, one of the strangest Japanese anime cartoons is *Panty & Stocking with Garterbelt*, which premiered in autumn 2010. For those who are interested, Panty is an incredibly promiscuous blonde who can turn her underwear into guns while Stocking is a goth who turns her stockings into swords. As for Garterbelt, well he's a priest with some strange fetishes. Their first enemy was a giant turd.

> 'You can't polish a turd (but you can roll it in glitter).'
>
> ANON

Did you know?

In 1889 there was breakthrough in chamber pot design – the addition of a handle. It was added, a contemporary report describes, 'to obviate the necessity for putting the thumb inside the vessel when holding the same, as is now generally the custom'.

Going to a public bathroom like a **man**

1 Walk slowly and proudly up to the bathroom.

2 Forcefully push open the door like you're a Wild-West gunslinger entering a saloon bar.

3 Enter the bathroom and quickly survey the room searching for the 'right' urinal, where's there's at least one empty space between you and the next man.

4 Approach the urinal at a brisk, confident pace, keeping your eyes straight ahead.

5 Unzip fly and relieve yourself as quickly as possible, still keeping your head and eyes fixed forward (the slightest sideways glance, however unintentional, will make your urinal neighbours think you're trying to check them out).

6 Shake it off.

7 Put it back in your trousers.

8 Carry out a courtesy wash, shaking your hands under a tap that may or not be dispensing water (soap unnecessary).

9 Attempt to dry hands for five to ten seconds. If you can't be bothered to use the hot air drier or paper towels, your clothes are just as effective.

10 Exit bathroom; do not look back.

NB Stages 6, 8 and 9 are optional. Stage 7 is not.

'Let's refrain from urinating in public.'

SIGN AT THE 1964 TOKYO OLYMPICS.

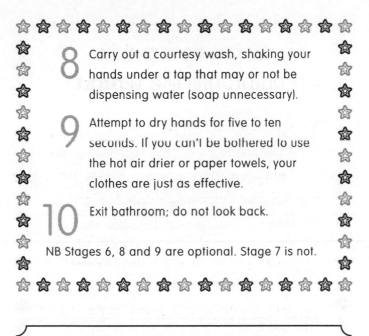

Did you know?

Separate male and female toilets were first recorded in Paris in 1739.

Going to a public bathroom like a **woman**

1 Enter bathroom and start checking each cubicle bowl, floor, walls and ceiling (in that order), deciding which one looks the cleanest – and nicest.

2 Enter your chosen cubicle ahead of the woman who walked into the bathroom behind you.

3 Lock the door.

4 If this other woman chooses 'your' cubicle, mutter 'bitch' or 'slut' under your breath, enter your second choice and lock the door.

5 Unlock and lock the door again. You want to be 100 per cent certain the cubicle is secure.

6 Hang your jacket and handbag on the door hook. If the toilet seat is 'up' go to stage 7. If not, go to stage 8.

7 Wrapping toilet paper all around your hand like an Andrex glove, lower the toilet seat onto the bowl.

8 Using toilet paper, wipe the seat at least twice. Throw the paper into the bowl.

9 Repeat stage 8 twice more. Throw the paper into the bowl.

10 Line the toilet seat with some toilet paper.

11 Add another layer to ensure that absolutely no piece of the seat will come into contact with your bare skin.

12 Repeat stage 5. You can't be too certain.

13 Start removing clothing, ensuring that none of it rests on the floor. If necessary, use the door hook.

14 Sit down gently on the toilet seat ensuring you don't disturb the toilet paper layer.

15 Carefully lean forward and repeat stage 5.

16 Relax and go.

17 Unroll the required amount of toilet paper, fold it into neat squares and wipe effectively until you're clean and dry.

18 Throw used toilet paper into the bowl, carefully holding it by clean parts.

19 Reversal of stage 13, ensuring that all clothing, in terms of order and appearance, looks exactly as it did when you first entered the bathroom.

20 Remove the toilet paper lining the seat and throw this into the toilet.

21 Flush.

22 Remove jacket from hook and put back on.

23 Remove handbag from hook and unlock door.

24 Walk to sink and turn on warm tap.

25 Hold hands under running water for at least thirty seconds.

26 Dispense soap and apply all over hands.

27 Repeat stage 26.

28 Rinse soap off hands under warm water for at least thirty seconds.

29 Look for paper towels and dry hands until every last trace of moisture has gone. If there are no paper towels hold hands under hot air drier for three minutes.

30 Proceed back to the driest sink and spread the contents of your handbag on the counter.

31 Look around at the other women in the bathroom and think caustic comments about their appearance and dress sense.

32 Reapply already perfect make-up for at least two minutes.

33 Replace the contents of your bag, taking the opportunity to reorganize the various pockets and compartments.

34 Glance in mirror again and reapply lipstick.

35 Walk out of bathroom, studying anyone you pass (see stage 31).

Pure genius!

The genius Leonardo da Vinci, while known as a great artist and inventor, was also very concerned about matters of hygiene. He designed houses with spiral staircases – not because of aesthetic or construction issues – but because he wanted to discourage residents from the common practice of urinating and defecating in the stairwells.

Did you know?

Before 1975 TV commercials for toilet paper in the United States had to refer to it as 'Bathroom Tissue'. The word 'toilet' was a six-letter word!

As used by . . .

The first two-ply soft toilet paper Andrex was originally developed as a paper handkerchief for gentlemen, and was initially sold exclusively in Harrods when it was launched in 1942. It became popular in the US when it was revealed that Hollywood stars of the day insisted on using it.

Toilet humour 22

An eighty-eight-year-old man had just had his annual check-up. As he put his clothes back on his doctor said, 'Well, for a man of your age you are in remarkable shape.'

The patient replied, 'Well, can't say I'm surprised. I live a good, clean, spiritual life and in return the Lord looks after me.'

The doctor asked, 'What makes you say that?'

The old man replied, 'Well, if I didn't live such a good life, then the Lord wouldn't turn the bathroom light on for me every time I get up in the middle of the night.'

'You mean to tell me', the doctor said, 'that when you get up in the night to go to the toilet, the Lord himself turns on the light for you?'

'Sure,' the old man said. 'He's been doing it for a number of years.'

The doctor was puzzled and didn't say anything else until the old man's wife came in for her own check-up a few days later.

'Your husband probably told you that he's in fine physical shape,' the doctor told her. 'But I'm slightly worried about his mental state. He told me that every night when he gets up to go to the bathroom, the Lord turns the light on for him.'

'Oh!' she exclaimed. 'So it's him who's been pissing in the fridge!'

A solid investment

Although it might sound like it, the Lloyds Bank Turd is not the nickname for a prominent chief executive, partly responsible for the financial crisis. Instead, it's the name given to a perfectly preserved 9-inch Viking stool believed to be over one thousand years old, and found in an archaeological dig beneath a branch of the bank in York.

Statistically speaking

2.6 billion people, nearly half the world's population, don't have access to toilets or proper sanitation.

Unprofessional conduct

Twenty-four-year-old Ebony Frew of Cleveland, Ohio, failed her driving test due to her examiner continually passing wind. According to Frew, this started as soon as he got in the car and continued throughout the test. By the time she had to demonstrate an emergency stop, the smell had rendered her half-unconscious and she crashed into the back of another vehicle. The examiner denied the allegations, blaming the smell in the car as 'exhaust fumes'.

Did you know?

After making a huge loss in 1990–91, KLM Royal Dutch Airlines decided to save 50,000 guilders a year by no longer printing a small aircraft motif on its airline toilet paper.

Pissed off!

The following anecdote was allegedly told on Jay Leno's show in July 1999. Jay walked into the audience, wanting to know the most embarrassing first date a woman had ever had. The winner recounted this story:

She'd just met a guy and, as a first date, he said he'd take her for a day's skiing. They had fun but it soon turned really, really cold and the roads were icing over so they decided to get back. Because of the freezing conditions the journey back took a lot longer than they anticipated and the girl really wanted to pee badly. She tried to keep it in but eventually they had to stop the car so she could get out and pee by the roadside.

Standing beside the car, she pulled down her snow pants and knickers but because the ground was icy, she had to steady herself against the car by resting a butt cheek against the rear bumper. She relieved herself while her date looked the other way. However, when she tried to pull her knickers and pants up, she realized that her butt had frozen to the metal bumper. Embarrassed as she'd just met this guy, the girl tried to slowly wriggle herself free without letting him know what had happened. She soon realized that she risked painfully pulling off a large part of skin unless she asked him for assistance.

Covering herself with her jacket to hide as much of her embarrassment as possible, she shouted for help and he went round to the back of the car to consider the situation. They had a real problem. It was getting colder, they were in the middle of nowhere and the only solution was to find a warm liquid that would slightly raise the temperature of the bumper. After considering every possible option they decided the only thing for it was urine. His. While she looked the other way, her date relieved himself and managed to pee her butt off the bumper.

She told Jay that on the rest of the trip back, there wasn't that much conversation . . .

Did you know?

The world's most expensive toilet paper is Renova. Manufactured from 100 per cent virgin pulp for maximum softness, it's three-ply and comes in six designer colours, including black. According to the manufacturers it has been through 'full dermatological tests to ensure that the level of hygiene meets the level of luxury' and offers a 'soft and silky experience'. You can buy it in the UK – approximately £8.50 for three rolls.

Toilet humour 23

Keith and Mac were drinking buddies who worked as aircraft mechanics at Glasgow airport. One day the airport was fogged in and they were as bored as hell, stuck in the hangar with nothing to do.

Keith said, 'Man, it's times like this that I could kill for a drink!'

'Me too,' said Mac. 'You know, I've heard that drinking aviation fuel gives you a real buzz. Something you'll never get with anything else.'

Making sure no one was looking, they poured themselves a few glasses of pure, high-octane jet fuel and proceeded to get completely smashed. They somehow managed to finish their shift and make their way home.

The next morning, Keith wakes up and is surprised at how good he feels. There's no hangover and no bad side effects. Just then the phone rings. It's Mac.

'Hey buddy, how do you feel this morning?'

Keith says, 'I feel great. How about you?'

Mac says, 'I feel great, too. No fuzzy head. No sickness.'

Keith says, 'Me too! That jet fuel is amazing. We ought to do this more often.'

'Yeah, well there's just one thing,' Mac says.

'What's that?' asks Keith.

'Have you farted yet?'

'No . . .'

'Well, don't!' says Mac. ''Cause I'm in Newcastle!'

Performance Fart

Meet the Manic Farter

The French baker Joseph Pujol (1857–1945) was better known for his flatulence than his flatbread, achieving fame as 'Le Pétomane' (an approximate translation is 'the manic farter'). In his youth, Joseph was able to suck air directly into his rectum so that he could fart at will (strictly speaking it wasn't actually farting since it didn't involve intestinal gases – but let's not quibble over this). Joseph developed this skill into a music-hall act and was soon enthralling audiences by imitating a cannon, a barking dog, a duck, an owl, a swarm of bees, a pig and a creaking door. It wasn't long before Joseph soon became the toast of Paris and one of the highest paid cabaret stars in the 1890s. He could also play a small flute inserted in his rectum, recreate and sustain any note from bottom A to top C and fart musical requests from the audience.

Performing in front of such luminaries as King Leopold II of Belgium and Edward, the Prince of Wales, Le Pétomane soon became an international star. For an encore he would insert a long rubber tube in his anus and place a lighted cigarette at the end. He would then draw on the cigarette and exhale smoke rings from his mouth.

On his deathbed at the age of eighty-eight, he was said to have farted the tune of 'The Last Post' – a showman to the very end.

Meet Mr Methane

The UK equivalent of Le Pétomane, and one of the few performing 'fartists' in the world, is Paul Oldfield, an ex-train driver who now performs under the stage name 'Mr Methane'. His act has included a farting rendition of 'God Save the Queen'. In 2009, he auditioned for *Britain's Got Talent* by farting 'The Blue Danube', but failed to make it through to the live finals. After being eliminated by all three judges Simon Cowell called him 'a vile, disgusting creature'.

Meet the Kumar

Rajiv Kumar from Madras, a station announcer for the Indian Rail Service, was sacked for using the PA system to broadcast himself breaking wind to the tune of Beethoven's *Fifth*. When asked to explain his actions, Kumar said, 'I like to entertain people. I often fart at parties and everyone likes it so I thought, why not at work?'

Did you know?

A way of discouraging dogs or cats to enter your garden is to urinate along the borders.

Practical jokes to play in public toilets

- Put cling film across the top of the toilet bowl, but under the seat. The person using the toilet will get their own back . . .

- Turn the hand drier nozzles into the upward position and fill them with talcum powder. As soon as they're turned on, the air will be filled with an unwelcome cloud of white dust.

- Fill a large washing-up liquid bottle with lemonade or ginger ale and take it into a cubicle with you. Squirt it erratically under the walls either side while yelling, 'My god, it's got a mind of its own! I just can't control it!'

- Take a small bottle of peanut butter (smooth or crunchy) into the cubicle with you and spread some onto a wad of toilet paper. Throw the paper under the next cubicle and say, 'Sorry. Can you kick that back to me please?'

- Make a loud farting noise with your hand and mouth then drop a marble on to the floor, saying, 'Shit! It blew my glass eye out!'

- When you've finished peeing in a urinal and you're shaking, make sure you hit the side of the urinal with the back of your hand. That way it sounds like you have a 10-pound penis.

- Grunt and strain really loudly for about thirty seconds; then, standing as high as you can, drop a large melon or grapefruit into the toilet bowl. Give a long, relaxed sigh.

- Suddenly announce, 'Humus. It reminds me of humus.' Pause, then say, 'Doesn't taste like it though.'

Did you know?

In 2007 Sim Jae-Duck of Korea constructed a house made to resemble a giant toilet. He called it 'haewoojae' which means 'a place where one can solve one's worries'. Sim built the house to call people's attention to the worldwide lack of toilets, particularly in developing countries.

The haunted toilet

New Yorker Richard Stern suffered a broken pelvis after being mysteriously sucked into his own lavatory. Rather than blame a freak accident involving water pressure or an airlock, Stern believes he is victim to a haunted toilet and the ghost of a dead plumber. It all began, Stern claims, when the plumber that he employed to fix a small leak was found dead on the job. Since then, the toilet has been behaving oddly. Pipes clank, the toilet whispers the plumber's name when Stern is trying to sleep, and he even claims to have seen a ghostly face in the bowl.

Toilet humour 24

Two men are in a gym locker room taking a shower when one notices the other has a huge cork stuck in his rear.

'I hope you don't mind me asking,' says the first man, 'But that cork looks really uncomfortable. Why don't you take it out?'

'I can't,' says the second man with more than a hint of sadness in his voice, 'It's stuck there permanently.'

'What happened?' asked the first man.

'Well, I was on holiday, walking along this beach when I tripped over this old oil lamp half buried in the sand. I knew the legend so I dug the lamp out, cleaned it off, then rubbed it. Next thing I knew there was this huge puff of smoke and a genie appeared. In a deep voice he said, "I am the genie of the lamp and I can grant you one wish." Unfortunately the first thing I said was, "No shit!"'

That's just gross!

☞ **In a dire emergency the Apache tribe were known to drink from their horses' bladders.**

The sit-down stick-up

Canadian storeowner Gerbert Huck of Vernon, British Colombia, was victim to a hold-up. A robber ran in, gun held aloft, and demanded that everyone stay where they were. However, before he had time to rifle the till, he was caught short in desperate need of the toilet. He ordered Gerbert, his staff, and customers to keep their hands up in the air while he used the staff bathroom. Everyone stayed silent; the only sounds were the robber's strains and groans as he relieved himself. After a while he emerged, completed his robbery and left.

Huck commented afterwards, 'We thought he might be looking at us through the keyhole. The last thing you want to do is upset a thief while he's on the toilet.'

Did you know?

If you were caught short in eighteenth-century Edinburgh you could defecate into a chamber pot carried by a 'John'. For a fee of a halfpenny he'd let you use the pot, covering your modesty by holding his large black cape around you.

Statistically speaking

Only 7 per cent of homes in Afghanistan have a flushing toilet, but 19 per cent have a television.

Lost in the loo

Japanese student Kando Kenasaki was using a public lavatory in a Tokyo suburb when he spotted a brown paper bag in the cubicle that contained the equivalent of £122,000. Being very honest, he stood on the seat and asked occupants in the adjacent cubicles if they'd lost any money but they all said no. He then asked people in all the other cubicles but they too said no. He was eventually asked to leave by the lavatory attendant, who thought he was soliciting. Kenasaki handed the money in to a police station but it was returned to him when no one made a claim.

Pleased with his windfall, Kenasaki commented, 'At first I thought the money might be some sort of novelty toilet paper.'

Death by dunny

As a result of his long-term drug abuse, Elvis Presley was severely constipated towards the end of his life and, because he was in the bathroom for hours at a time, tended to do a lot of his reading there. When he did die sitting on the toilet, he was engrossed in a book about the Turin Shroud.

Other notable names reported to have died in the bathroom include:

- Actress Judy Garland (1969, drug overdose)
- Novelist Evelyn Waugh (1966, heart failure)
- Comedian Lenny Bruce (1966, drug overdose)
- Actor Charles Chaplin Jnr (1968, brain embolism)
- Singer Jim Morrison (1971, drug overdose)
- *Top Gun* producer Don Simpson (1996, drug overdose)

Did you know?

A rat can tread water for three days after being flushed down a toilet, returning to the building via the same route.

Are you 'pee shy'?

Do you find it difficult to urinate in a public lavatory surrounded by other men? If so, you might be suffering from Avoidance Paruresis, a condition thought to affect about 7 per cent of men. Also known as 'bashful bladder' or 'pee shy' syndrome, it's a psychological problem but with physical effects; anxiety causes the sphincter muscle that controls the bladder to clench so tight that urination is impossible. About 1 million men suffer from it so severely that they are unable to use a toilet outside their own home.

The International Paruresis Association is a support group for sufferers. Members drink considerable amounts of water, are paired up with a 'Pee Buddy' and go to public restrooms, building up confidence to be able to urinate in busier and busier toilets. The Association's ultimate aim is to get members to urinate in the restrooms of a packed sports stadium.

Did you know?

Most toilets flush in the key of E Flat.

❖ ❖ ❖ ❖ ❖ ❖ ❖ ❖ ❖ ❖ ❖ ❖ ❖ ❖ ❖ ❖

Toilet humour **25**

Why is it that people point to their wrist when they ask for the time, but they don't point to their crotch when they ask where the bathroom is?

❖ ❖ ❖ ❖ ❖ ❖ ❖ ❖ ❖ ❖ ❖ ❖ ❖ ❖ ❖ ❖

It's a record!

GREATEST URINE PROJECTION

Peter Clarke of Springfield, Illinois, holds both the horizontal and vertical records. In January 1991 his streams reached the staggering distance of 21 feet 7 inches and a height of 15 feet 3 inches. Peter retired from public performances the following year after severely rupturing his bladder, a result of his world record attempts.

LONGEST URINATION

The longest recorded and verified urination is attributed to David Lyons of Glasgow who, in May 1984, after preparing himself with 10 pints of cider, peed for an astonishing 24 minutes 46 seconds.

LARGEST TURD

The largest verified example of human faeces was produced by Carl Simms of Dallas, Texas in January 1989. It took him over two hours and the resulting stool was 12 feet 2 inches in length, with what was described as a 'remarkably consistent width'. Simms was subsequently banned from 134 public washrooms in the state.

WIDEST STOOL

The widest stool verified was produced by Peter James of Bradford (date unknown). This measured 4.5 inches in diameter. The record-breaking specimen was later preserved in alcohol.

MOST CONSTIPATED

The most constipated person on medical record is Henry Morton Williamson of London. In 1905 he went for eight months and sixteen days without a bowel movement, a result of a painful anal fissure. Due to his self-imposed toilet exile, Mr Williamson died from a strangulated hernia and ruptured stomach. The coroner later found 58 lb of faecal matter in his swollen intestines.

Did you know?

Adult men tend to pee in a narrower stream than adult women due to changes brought about by sex and/or childbirth. This fact was used centuries ago to test virginity. If a woman peed like a man then she was thought to be a virgin.

Did you know?

The downstairs Gents at the Queen's Head pub in Stockport measures just 17 inches (43 cm) wide. Not surprisingly, one 25-stone customer got completely stuck and had to be rescued by the fire brigade.

LOUDEST FART

The loudest farts ever recorded are attributed to David Baker of Rochester, New York. These measured 84 decibels over 2.6 seconds (that's louder than an alarm clock heard at 2 feet).

LONGEST FART

The longest fart, however, belonged to Bernard Clemmens of London in December 1991. It officially lasted for a staggering 2 minutes 42 seconds.

FASTEST FART LIGHTING

'Sam' Yakkashima of Tokyo was filmed in May 1991 setting light to eighty-nine farts in under one minute. The farts themselves were provided by his eight assistants.

Statistically speaking

Up to half of all adult men and a quarter of adult women don't wash their hands after visiting the toilet.

Euphemisms:
21 Number Ones

1. Wipe the dew off the lily

2. Point Percy at the porcelain

3. Tapping a kidney

4. Wring the rattlesnake

5. Water the horses

6. Syphon the python

7. Splash the pirate

8. Splash my boots

9. Put out a fire

10. Squeeze the lemon

11. Return the beer I rented

12. Train Terrence on the Terracotta

13. Drain the radiator

14. Make my bladder gladder

15. Shake hands with the President

16. Shake hands with the wife's best friend

17. Shake hands with the guy I enlisted with

18. Shake hands with the unemployed

19. Drain the dragon

20. Drain the main vein

21. Drain the crankcase

Euphemisms:
22 Number Twos

1. Launch the big ship
2. Drop the kids off at the pool
3. Serve up some McButt nuggets
4. Take The Browns to the Super Bowl
5. Take a pit stop
6. Go for a Donald Trump
7. Lengthen the spine
8. Take a Shatner
9. Free the chocolate hostages
10. Walk Winnie (i.e. the Pooh)
11. Make a deposit
12. Dispatch the cargo
13. Ride the porcelain bus
14. Imitate the Play-Doh Fun Factory
15. Cut some brown rope
16. Send a brown fax
17. Crack the dam on the rectal river
18. Play the role of King Poo-Poo-Rama on his throne
19. Post a letter
20. Back the big brown bus out of the garage
21. Bake brownies
22. Download 5MB (or 10MB for a larger turd)

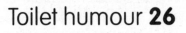

Toilet humour 26

After a few drinks in a bar a man and woman start to get very competitive, each one bragging that they can outdo the other at anything. Eventually the man decides to put his money where his mouth is.

'Pissing,' the man says. '£50 says I can piss further than you!'

'You're on!' says the woman to his surprise. 'But I want one concession.'

'What's that?' he asks, knowing he could out-piss the women in any situation.

'No hands,' the woman answers.

Crappy airlines!

Contrary to popular belief, airlines do not dump toilet waste out of the aircraft while they are flying; it's kept in holding tanks until the planes land and then pumped out into ground service vehicles (known in the industry as 'honey carts') and taken to a treatment facility. That wasn't always the case; the first passenger planes weren't pressurized and the first toilets were glorified potties (and it was easy to open doors and windows).

That's not to say that waste never falls from the skies. Faulty valves or seals on the holding tanks mean that waste has been known to leak out, freeze and then plummet to earth like a missile. Known euphemistically as 'blue ice', this frozen waste has been known to fall to earth in lumps from the size of small rocks to basketballs, causing damage to houses but, so far, no authenticated human injuries.

Royal Flush

Once, when the Royal Yacht *Britannia* went into dock for a refit, the mahogany toilet seats were all removed and replaced. It's said that, rather than dispose of them, they found their way to a local carpenter who had a lucrative sideline transforming them into presentation cigarette and cigar boxes with a certain mystery attached . . . which royal bottoms had graced the wood with their presence.

Piss rich not piss poor

In the early eighteenth century it was possible to buy chamber pots featuring the face of Henry Sacheverell, an unloved politician and radical preacher. So successful was this design that the Clapton-based manufacturer was able to build himself a grand house, which he proudly named Piss-Pot Hall.

Brace yourself

In 2009, following an engine failure 150 feet over Thun Field in Washington State, the sixty-seven-year-old solo pilot of a Cessna 182 began an emergency descent, eventually crash-landing on a row of portable toilets. The fortunate pilot walked away from the crash. A spokesman later commented that the toilets 'had kind of cushioned things'.

Privy Playtime: **Toilet Maze**

Help the turd find its way from the toilet to the river . . .

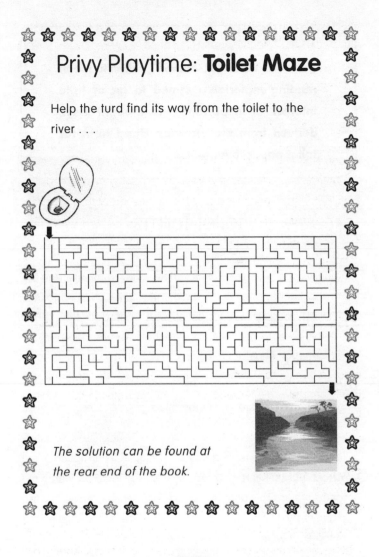

The solution can be found at the rear end of the book.

Did you know?

The word 'bumf' (or, 'bumph'), taken to mean reading materials deemed to be of little interest or importance, is thought have derived from the Victorian slang term for toilet paper, 'bum fodder'.

Toilet Terms

BOG

Originally, 'bog' was used to describe an open cesspit and the word was later applied to the rudimentary toilet connected to it. The word 'bog-house' for toilet was recorded from 1670 while the verb 'to bog', i.e. to defecate, was recorded in the late nineteenth century.

LOO

The origins of 'loo' are lost in the mists of time. Here, however, are several theories:

- It derives from the term 'gardyloo', which is a corruption of the French phrase 'gardez l'eau', loosely translated as 'watch out for the water'. This phrase was used in medieval times to warn passers-by when chamber pots were about to be emptied out of top-floor windows on to the streets below.

- It comes from nautical terminology. The standard nautical pronunciation of leeward was 'looward'. Early ships were not fitted with toilets but the crew would urinate over the leeward (sheltered) side of their vessel. If they used the windward side, the urine would usually be blown back on deck.

- It's also claimed that an early British toilet manufacturer produced a cistern model named 'Waterloo' to celebrate victory at the Battle of Waterloo. To go to the toilet became known as 'going to the Waterloo' which was then abbreviated to simply 'going to the 'loo'.

- It derives from the French word 'lieu' meaning 'place', as in 'that place'. Some seventeenth-century English architectural plans denote the bathroom as 'le lieu'.

- It comes from the old European practice of referring to the bathroom as 'Room 100'. When written down, the number '100' looks like the word 'loo'.

- When church sermons lasted for several hours, women used to conceal and use 'pee bottles' discreetly under their voluminous skirts. The French slang name for these vessels was the 'bordaloue', named after the Jesuit priest Louis Bordaloue whose sermons were described as 'bladder-strainingly long'. Bordaloue became shortened to 'loue'.

- A less-believable origin is that it's short for 'Lady Louisa', Louisa being the unpopular wife of the nineteenth-century Earl of Lichfield. In 1867, while the couple was staying with friends, two jokers in the party removed the name card from her bedroom door and instead stuck it on the door of the bathroom. The other guests then referred jokingly as 'going to Lady Louisa'. Louisa was soon shortened to loo and the word spread among the masses.

Did you know?

There is a Swedish brand of toilet paper called Krapp.

KHAZI/KARZY/KHARSIE

There are two schools of thought. The first is that it derives from the nineteenth-century Cockney word 'carsey', which means a privy (possibly deriving before that from 'casa', the Italian for house). The other explanation is that it comes from a British Army insult, originating from officers stationed in India who took a dislike to the habits of the Khasi people from the Khasia hills on the northern frontier of India.

CRAP

This word, a slang term for faeces, does not, as many people believe, derive from the name of plumbing pioneer Thomas Crapper. Instead, it is a fifteenth-century English word derived from Old Dutch that means dregs, cast-offs and residue. The first recorded use of the word in the sense 'to defecate' dates back to 1846, when Thomas Crapper was only ten years old.

JOHN

While no one knows definitively, the American euphemism for a toilet is thought to derive from John Harington, the British nobleman credited with inventing the first flushing toilet in 1596. Another explanation is that John is a derivation of the term 'Jakes' or 'the Jakes', medieval English slang for a latrine.

DUNNY

The Australian slang for a toilet (usually an outhouse) derives from the old English dialect word 'dunnekin', meaning a dung house or cesspit.

JERRY

This English slang for a chamber pot is thought to have two derivations. The more widely believed is that it's an abbreviation of Jeroboam, a large bottle of champagne with the capacity of about four ordinary bottles – the name reflects the capacity of a chamber pot. Others claim that it refers to the biblical prophet Jeremiah who had a prophetic vision involving a potter. From potter to pot to chamber pot . . .

CAN

This Americanism possibly refers to non-flushing toilets that had a removable can or container under the seat so that waste could be easily emptied.

Did you know?

Urban myth states that urinating on a jellyfish sting will neutralize the poison, a scenario acted out in the *Friends* show 'The One with the Jellyfish', as well as in an episode of the reality show *Survivor*. At best, this method is ineffective and in some cases may actually make the injury worse since urine can activate venom remaining at the site of the sting.

Movements for his movement

Lord Baden-Powell, founder of the Boy Scouts movement, believed that to be healthy and strong, it was important to be 'regular' and to have what he called a 'rear' daily without fail. If the scout had difficulty going he recommended drinking plenty of water and practising 'body-twisting' exercises.

Ladies and gentlemen . . .

According to *Private Eye*, Cheltenham Spa council voted to change the signs on the toilets from 'Men' and 'Women' to 'Ladies' and 'Gentlemen' in order to 'attract a better class of person' to their lavatories.

Toilet philosophy

Confucius says:

Man who stand on toilet is high on pot.

Man who scratches ass should not bite fingernails.

Man who eat many prunes get good run for money.

Man who farts in church sits in own pew.

Spoilt for choice

The Pentagon in the US has 284 bathrooms – twice as many as it really needs. When it was built in the 1940s, the state of Virginia still had segregation laws requiring government buildings to have separate toilet facilities for whites and blacks.

Toilet humour **27**

A colonel was dictating some correspondence to his secretary when she noticed that his fly was open. She didn't know how to mention this diplomatically so she decided to use language he'd understand. She leaned towards him and whispered, 'Sir, did you know that your barracks door is open?'

The colonel frowned so she repeated herself.

He frowned and pondered a bit and then the penny dropped.

'Ahh,' he said and, slightly embarrassed, adjusted his zip.

Later that day he decided to have some fun with his secretary and called her back into his office.

'By the way, Miss Smith,' he smiled. 'When you noticed that the barracks door was open before, did you happen to see a soldier standing to attention?'

Without batting an eyelid the secretary replied, 'No, sir. But I did see a small disabled veteran slumped on two worn-out duffle bags.'

That's just gross!

The medieval Feast of Fools involved actors dressed as clowns or women eating excrement and throwing it at bystanders from dung carts.

Pee shooter

During the American Civil War, urine was distilled into nitre, an important component in the manufacture of gunpowder. Confederate supporters would go from house to house, collecting the contents of chamber pots to help the Southern cause.

A contemporary poem ends with the lines: '. . . But 'tis an awful idea . . . gunpowdery and cranky/That when a lady lifts her skirts, she's killing off a Yankee!'

Did you know?

Hermann Goering, Commander-in-Chief of the Luftwaffe, refused to use toilet paper, insisting on using soft white cotton handkerchiefs that he bought in bulk.

Toilet humour **28**

A Jewish couple had an unfortunate incident when, early one morning, the drowsy wife got up to take a pee and forgot the seat was up. The result was that she slipped into the toilet bowl and got wedged in, her open legs sticking right up in front of her.

Her screams awoke her husband who rushed in, but no matter how much he pulled, he couldn't free her. As a very last resort he phoned an emergency plumber. Eventually the plumber arrived and as the husband was walking him from the front door to the bathroom he suddenly realized that his wife was completely naked and exposed in a very humiliating way. Thinking fast he ran ahead of the plumber, dashed into the bathroom and put his skullcap between her legs to cover her.

The plumber walked into the bathroom, took a long look at the sight before him and shook his head. Turning to the husband he said, 'Well I think I can save your wife but the rabbi's a goner.'

It's a dirty job but someone's got to do it

Next time you say you've got a shit job, spare a thought for the sixteenth-century equivalent of Dyno-Rod, the gong scourers. The word 'gong' comes from 'gung', which in turn is a derivative of 'dung'. For gong scourers, the day was spent sometimes up to the waist in human waste, usually working as part of a team.

One of the main problems facing the City of London during its rapid expansion at this time was the disposal of sewage. Human waste would either end up in the Thames or was deposited in large cesspits. It was when these cesspits became full that you called in the gong scourers. They worked exclusively at night by candlelight and removed the effluent by hand, depositing it in a large horse-drawn vat for disposal outside the City. The top layer of the waste was liquid and emptied by bucket. Beneath this was a solid, thick sludge that had to be dug out. As you can imagine, the stench was unbearable and many gong scourers died from suffocation. When tobacco became available, many gong scourers adopted smoking, just to keep away the fumes.

On one occasion, a gong scourer, rather than cart the waste away, emptied it into a drain. As punishment he was made to sit up to his neck in a vat of effluent in Golden Lane, London. A sign around his neck told passers-by of his crime.

Statistically speaking

The odds are 1 in 10,000 that you will receive a toilet-related injury.

Holding it in

The famed Danish astronomer Tycho Brae (1546–1601) quite literally had his head in the stars just before an important state banquet. He forgot to go to the lavatory, an act that would have disastrous consequences. At the time it was considered impolite and insulting to the host if you left the table before the meal was over. Brae desperately wanted to go but had to suffer in silence. The result of his good manners was a burst bladder, followed by a painful death eleven days later.

Toilet humour **29**

Q: Why did the blonde throw bread down the toilet?

A: To feed the toilet duck.

Your presence is requested ...

King Ferdinand I of Naples suffered from constipation but insisted on the presence of his visitors and courtiers while he strained himself on the royal toilet. One of these was the Emperor Joseph of Austria who noted, 'We made conversation for more than half an hour and I believe he would still be there if a terrible stench had not convinced us that it was all over.'

Much more recently, President Lyndon Johnson upset his staff and reporters with his habit of continuing a conversation in the bathroom whenever he was caught short. Many of his 'guests' felt rather uneasy at watching the President go about his official business and this became a great source of amusement to him. One high-ranking member of staff insisted on keeping his back towards the President, which made having a conversation difficult. Johnson insisted that he came nearer but rather than turn around the man walked backwards, one slow step at a time. Johnson later commented, 'For a moment I thought he was going to back right into me. It certainly made me wonder how that man had made it so far in the world.'

Accidents will happen

Twenty-one-year-old Kitano Koshiki of Tokyo died while bowing to a toilet. The incident happened while he was waiting for an interview at a major Japanese bank. Koshiki arrived early and wanted to practise bowing in front of his interviewer to ensure he delivered a perfect greeting – and the most private place he could find to do this was a toilet cubicle.

A bank employee who happened to be at the urinals at the time said, 'I heard a soft voice say several times, "Thank you, dear sir, I am honoured to be in your presence." The last time he said it there was a loud clunk – then the sound of someone falling to the floor.' Bank security was called and they broke open the cubicle door to find Koshiki dead, the result of a fractured skull. His tearful mother later commented, 'He died in a bank, which is as he would have wanted it.'

Have you been to the Bleeping Bathroom?

In the US, an Atlantic City hotel has a novel way of ensuring its employees are hygienic. They are all issued with badges fitted with electronic sensors which bleep unless they spend at least fifteen seconds at the sink after they've been to the bathroom.

Did you know?

Ninety per cent of pharmaceuticals taken by people are excreted through urination. A recent study by the EPA found trace elements of pain relievers, antibiotics, cholesterol-reducing drugs and even antidepressants in fish.

Burton's bladder

It's well known that an excess of alcohol can have a very detrimental effect on bladder control. Testament to this was Richard Burton's performance in *Henry V* at London's Old Vic theatre in 1953. After drinking several pints of beer during the interval, Burton found himself caught short in the middle of the stage so he turned his back on the audience and relieved himself in his chain mail costume. Being chain mail, the urine leaked out on to the stage and flowed into the hot footlights. The ensuing cloud of toxic gas meant that people in the first ten rows of the stalls had to vacate their seats.

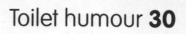

Toilet humour **30**

Q: What's in the toilet of the *Starship Enterprise*?

A: The captain's log.

Holy faeces!

In one of his more lighthearted moments, Pope Alexander IV (1199–1261) recounted a story in which a wayward priest attempted to molest a parishioner in the confession box. To escape his desires she told him that a romantic liaison outside the church premises would be better. In advance of this she sent him a home-made pie as a token of her love – a pie filled with her own excrement. Rather than eat it as she had hoped, the priest gave the pie to his bishop as a gift. He was soon relieved of his priestly duties.

Privy Playtime:
Find the poet

The letters of **TOILETS** can be rearranged into which well-known poet and playwright?

Answer at the rear end of the book.

An Englishman's home

Toilets in medieval castles were known as 'garderobes' – small stone seats set into recesses in external walls. Often located in towers, the waste would fall directly into the moat below. The moat's use as a cesspit, while making living in a castle quite unpleasant, also discouraged invading soldiers from wading or swimming through it to gain access to the castle walls.

The word 'garderobe' actually means clothes closet, since the small space resembled a dressing room.

Luminous loo paper and other genuine novelties

Toilet paper doesn't have to be boring white or plain pastel. There's a whole range of novelty designs to make your bathroom visit more interesting:

JOB APPLICATION
Write your CV in the WC – this toilet paper has sections to enter your contact information, education and career details.

SUDOKU
You know that joke about working it out with a pencil . . . Well, now you really can.

MONEY
Feel like a millionaire each time you wipe – each sheet on the roll resembles a dollar bill.

GLOW IN THE DARK
Find your way during a power cut with this luminous loo paper.

ORIGAMI

Each sheet has complete instructions on how to fold your own paper crane.

MANGA

The Japanese brand Banbix has joined forces with a renowned manga artist to present a comic on a roll. See the story unwind as you unwind . . .

MONOGRAMMED

Keep one step ahead of the Joneses by having your initials embossed in gold on this super-soft paper.

HORROR STORY

Scare yourself shitless with this horror tale on a toilet roll, written by Koji Suzuki, author of *The Ring*.

CHEESE GRATER

Ever wanted to wipe yourself with a cheese grater? Me too! With this realistic-looking toilet paper you can have the experience without the pain.

Did you know?

The urine of eunuchs, if drunk, was thought to make barren women fertile.

Toilet humour 31

Q: What do the clitoris, wedding anniversaries and toilets have in common?

A: Men usually miss them.

Bombs away!

In October 1965, to commemorate the 6 millionth pound of explosives to be dropped on North Vietnam, Commander Clarence W. Stoddard Jr delivered a very special bomb from his Skyraider aircraft . . . an old toilet. The toilet came from Stoddard's vessel, the aircraft carrier USS *Midway*. It was damaged and was about to be thrown overboard when someone had the bright idea of rescuing it, adding tail fins, and finding way to safely mount it on an aircraft.

The toilet was secretly fixed to Stoddard's plane and as he taxied to take off, fellow crewmen positioned themselves so they obscured the view of the ship's captain. After he was airborne, the bridge radioed with a sense of alarm, 'What the hell was that on Flight 572's right wing?'

The result of the toilet falling on North Vietnamese troops was not reported although it was said to 'whistle all the way down'.

Did you know?

The first public toilets were installed in France in 1824.

BBC WCs

It was reported that last year the BBC spent nearly £400,000 on lawyers' fees responding to various Freedom of Information requests. As a public body, the BBC has to be as open as it can. However, as Director General Mark Thompson commented, 'It's still painful to spend public money that could be invested on programmes answering weighty questions like, "How many toilets do you have in BBC Television Centre?"'

Toilet humour 32

Q: Why did the fly fall off the urinal?

A: It got pissed off.

'There are three things you need in life: respect for all kinds of life, a nice bowel movement on a regular basis and a blue blazer.'

ROBIN WILLIAMS IN *THE FISHER KING*

When in Rome . . .

- One of the very first recorded examples of public toilets were the large vases, or *gastras*, found alongside Roman roads for travellers to relieve themselves in.

- It's a misconception that all Romans enjoyed toilets and good sanitation. Only the richest citizens could afford the permits to connect their homes to the city sewers. Everyone else had to make do with chamber pots emptied into cesspits or public latrines.

- Romans who couldn't afford a chamber pot at home often urinated in a corner of their shared building when no one was looking. This is thought to have given rise to the expression 'not having a pot to piss in'.

- To discourage graffiti in Rome's public latrines, the walls were usually covered with depictions of gods and goddesses. It was a very serious offence to deface these images.

- Described as a tyrannical monster, the Roman Emperor Commodus (who ruled from AD 180 to 192) partied his way through life, entertaining his entourage of three hundred girls and three hundred boys. Given his various acts of decadence, cruelty and vanity (and his penchant for wearing women's clothing) it's difficult to know exactly when Commodus 'lost it', but his decision to start eating human excrement that had been mixed with the most expensive foods at his feasts would have been a good indication. (NB his name has nothing to do with the commode.)

- A group of Roman soldiers were ordered to build a sewer and, fearing that they had disgraced themselves by this act, committed mass suicide.

- The Roman baths of Caracalla could accommodate 1,600 bathers at one time. In the early twentieth century, the baths' design was used as the inspiration for several modern structures, including Pennsylvania Station in New York City.

- A urine tax was imposed by Emperor Nero in around AD 60 – but on the collectors, not the producers. Tanners and laundry workers used to collect urine from public toilets, using the ammonia for curing leather and bleaching togas. This was such a good source of income that Nero's successor, Vespasian, continued the practice. When his own son, Titus, complained about the vulgar nature of the urine tax, Vespasian is alleged to have held up a gold coin in front of him and said, 'Non olet.' ('This doesn't stink.')

Fishy-sounding toilet

Ever wished your toilet tank was glass and contained live fish? Well, you should order a Tanquarium. Combining a toilet tank and an aquarium, the manufacturers claim the device can upgrade even the smallest bathroom to an attraction. The fish share the same water that's used for flushing but an innovative vacuum device ensures they can't be flushed out. According to the manufacturers, fish have lived safely in the device for two years. Flushing keeps the water clean; all you need to do is feed them. At the time of writing the Tanquarium can be yours for $430. See www.tanquarium.com.

The idea of displaying fish in the toilet tank isn't a new one. The Café du Trésor in Paris apparently has a similar (but less ingenious) device, with fish being kept in an inner glass tank that isn't affected by the cistern flushing.

Did you know?

It's claimed that running a pencil around the palm of your hand anticlockwise can stop the urge to pee.

A restaurant that soon fills up

At the Modern Toilet diner in Taipei guests sit on converted toilets, eat from mini plastic toilet bowls and wipe their hands and mouths using toilet rolls hung above their tables. According to owner Wang Tzi-wei, the diner attracts customers aged between fifteen and thirty-five. 'Older people', he said, 'just wouldn't get it.' Themed restaurants are popular in Taipei, with eateries resembling prisons and hospitals being among the more creative.

Although the unusual Modern Toilet diner has proved extremely popular with its younger clientele, it seems not everyone is impressed. One local mother commented, 'My son thought it was disgusting and didn't know if he could finish his food!'

NB As you might imagine, the Modern Toilet is part of a chain . . .

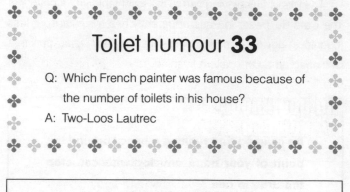

Toilet humour 33

Q: Which French painter was famous because of the number of toilets in his house?

A: Two-Loos Lautrec

Statistically speaking

According to a 2010 UK survey, 25 per cent of us use our mobile phones while on the toilet to chat, text, email or update Facebook.

Pop-up peeing

Dutch company UriLift manufactures 'pop-up' urinals that are becoming popular in city centres across Europe. Usually installed to reduce incidents of clubbers and drinkers urinating in the streets, the public toilets retract underground when not in use, usually rising to the surface between 10 p.m. and 6 a.m. Self-cleaning, the toilets are basically maintenance-free.

Going underground

An underground Edwardian public convenience at Shepherds Bush Green in London is now a trendy venue that hosts live music, comedy, club nights and also art exhibitions. Called Ginglik, the former toilet was built to serve the spectators of the

1908 Olympic Games at nearby White City, but was converted into the current venue in 2002. Acclaimed by *The Sunday Times* as 'one of London's coolest bars', performers have included Robin Williams, Jimmy Carr, Harry Hill, Frank Skinner and Paolo Nutini.

Did you know?

Dentists have recommended that tooth-brushes be kept at least 6 feet away from a toilet to avoid being contaminated by air-borne particles after a flush.

A very public toilet

In December 2003, in an effort to challenge the curiosity and bravery of people passing London's Tate Britain gallery, an artist, Monica Bonvicini, created a usable public toilet in a cube made from one-way mirrored glass. The work, entitled *Don't Miss A Sec*, using a stainless steel prison toilet as a historical reference, enabled people to use the toilet and look at onlookers, without being visible themselves.

A spokeswoman for the artist said, 'It will arouse curiosity because people can come and use it, although there is a question of whether people will feel comfortable doing so. They may be wary of desecrating a work of art or may be uneasy that because they can see out, other people can see in.'

Toilet humour 34

While his wife is out a man decides to take the opportunity to catch up with some DIY jobs, one of which is revarnishing the wooden toilet seat.

His wife comes home early and before he even knows she's back, she gets stuck fast to the toilet. No amount of pulling will free her so they decide to drive to the local A & E department to see if they have some sort of solvent. The husband unscrews the toilet seat and covers his wife with his overcoat to hide her embarrassment.

Eventually it's time to see a doctor. The woman removes the coat then bends down in front of him so he can see her dilemma.

'Doctor, have you seen anything like this before?' asks the husband.

'Well, yes,' the doctor replies, 'But never framed.'

Did you know?

The court official whose task it was to administer the Pharaoh's enema basked in the grand title of 'Shepherd to the Royal Anus'.

A brief history of toilet paper

1391	toilet paper first produced in China for the Emperor's use
1596	invention of the flushing toilet by Sir John Harington
1700s	widely available newspaper becomes a popular choice for toilet paper
1710	invention of the bidet
1857	first factory-made toilet paper sold in the US in packets of five hundred sheets
1879	first toilet paper sold on rolls available in US
1894	the Sears general merchandise catalogue first becomes available, commonly used as toilet paper in rural America
1897	first perforated toilet paper on a roll becomes readily available in the US
1900	plumbing improvements in the Victorian era lead to the widespread adoption of the flushing toilet and, in Europe, the bidet, increasing demand for toilet paper
1930s	Sears begins publishing its catalogue on less absorbent glossy paper, making it far less suitable as toilet tissue
1942	the first two-ply toilet paper manufactured by St Andrew's paper mill in England
1943	novelty toilet paper is printed with images of Hitler, Hirohito and Mussolini
1957	coloured toilet paper introduced
1980	invention of the paperless toilet in Japan
1990–1	US troops camouflage tanks with toilet paper in Operation Desert Storm

1990s	toilet paper containing herbal ingredients such as aloe begins to be marketed in the US
1990s	in the UK, Andrex sells the first moist toilet tissue
2010	First tube-free toilet paper introduced in the US

A toilet by any other name

Many late-nineteenth-century and early-twentieth-century toilets had names that were evocative of their flushing power. These included the Avalanche, the Cascade, the Climax, the Colossal, the Deluge, the Maelstrom, the Speedwell, the Tornado, the Torrent and the Vortex.

There was also the Cedric, the Clencher and the Monkey. Go figure!

Did you know?

In a survey on what would be the most important necessity to have on a desert island, almost half the respondents chose toilet paper ... more than those who nominated food.

Crap like a king

For those who like to go to the toilet like a king, look no further than the Herbeau 'Dagobert' Wooden Toilet Throne, a snip at just $14,000. Named after an eighth-century French monarch, the solid ash toilet houses an ornately decorated porcelain bowl, an ashtray and a candleholder. When the lid is lifted it plays 'Le bon roi Dagobert' ('The good king Dagobert'). The pull chain flushes the toilet and rings a bell to let your servants know that their wiping services are now required.

Statistically speaking

A salmonella germ can pass through twenty-eight sheets of toilet paper.

The turd as a unit of weight

According to a study (albeit a spurious one), the average US turd weighs 2.2 pounds, which, coincidentally, is exactly 1 kilogram. This fact has not gone unnoticed by proponents of a new system of weight measurement that would be a halfway house between the imperial and metric systems – the turd system. Like the metric method, measurement would be on a base ten structure, so you'd start with a turd and then progress to a centiturd (one hundred turds) and a milliturd (one thousand turds). Following this logic, a turd would be composed of one thousand microturds.

NB On this basis, Piers Morgan would weigh about seventy-eight turds, which shows the accuracy of the system.

That's just gross!

Native Indians in Bogotá, Colombia, used urine instead of salt to season their food.

Toilet humour 35

Three men in a nursing home were discussing the problems of ageing.

'Sixty is the worst age to be,' said a sixty-year-old. 'I always feel like I have to pee but most of the time I stand at the toilet and absolutely nothing comes out.'

'That's nothing!' said the seventy-year-old man. 'When you're my age, you can't take a dump anymore. I eat bran cereal or take laxatives then I sit on the loo all day and still nothing comes out!'

'Actually,' said the eighty-year-old, 'Eighty is the worst of all. When you're my age you take a piss every morning at seven followed by a shit at seven-thirty.'

'What's wrong with that?' asked the first man.

'I don't wake up 'til eight.'

Silent but deadly

Dr Grant Evans, a prominent obstetrician in Kansas, retired in 1986 due to health problems. Following abdominal surgery, he suffered from severe and very odorous farting, which he tried to alleviate by burning matches to cover the smell. In 1987, Dr Evans was admitted to the psychiatric unit of Wesley Medical Center, Wichita where he was being treated for major depression with melancholia. On 11 April that year he received fatal burns while seated on the toilet in his hospital room. Investigations proved that the fire had started in the crotch of his pyjamas, possibly as a result of carelessly dropping one of the matches lit to disguise his flatulence. His widow Arelene made a claim for $300,000 under her late husband's life insurance, however the insurance company Provident denied the claim on the basis that Dr Evan's death was the result of an intentionally self-inflicted injury, i.e. a suicide, and was not covered by the policy.

Arlene took Provident to the Kansas Supreme Court in 1991 and won her case on the basis of his history of trying to cover the smell of his farts and the fact that no one thinking of committing suicide would intentionally set fire to their crotch when there were many other less painful and more certain methods.

Statistically speaking

Ten per cent of all Americans still rely on an outhouse.

Privy Playtime: **Loo Quiz**

Find the one word that means each of the following (NB You'll find the word 'loo' in each of the answers):

1. Depressingly dark
2. A single-masted sailing vessel
3. Reserved and emotionally distant
4. Plundering, usually during a riot
5. Inuit house
6. Slang word for a crazy person
7. Notoriously hot curry
8. Deluge
9. Sponge used for washing
10. Pub lounge bar
11. Round or oval shape in handwriting
12. Loud noise or confusion
13. Personal possession, usually with a sentimental value, passed down through families
14. A spectator; someone who watches
15. Lowest horizontal surface of a room
16. Spanish gold coin loved by pirates
17. Pages that can be easily removed from a binder
18. Weakness or exception in a law
19. Old term for women's large pants
20. Fluid delivering nutrients around the body

Answers can be found at the rear end of the book.

Did you know?

The word 'urine' was first recorded in the fourteenth century. Before that, the accepted word for the substance was 'piss'. It is believed that the word 'piss' fell out of use and was thought vulgar because of its use by lower class characters in Chaucer's *The Canterbury Tales*.

It started here ...

Mesopotamia is known as the Cradle of Civilization but, according to one historian, it should also be acclaimed as the Seat of Sanitation. The Sumerians ruled the region from about 3000 BC and their leader, Sargon I, was said to have built the first ever private toilets in his palace. 'Toilets' might be too grand a word as they consisted of horseshoe-shaped seats located over a cesspit, but at least they were preferable to the usual undignified practice of squatting over large earthenware pots.

The first flush toilets were said to have been invented by the Minoans, the ancient Crete civilization that flourished from around 2700 to 1500 BC. The Palace of Knossos, built by King Minos, included a device that collected rainwater and channelled it through an ingenious system of terracotta pipes, flushing away the contents of the palace latrines.

NB This has nothing to do with the poker hand Royal Flush.

> 'Making movies is better than cleaning toilets.'
> KLAUS KINSKI

Biblical bogs

The Pharaohs of Ancient Egypt believed they were descended from gods and, in an effort to distance themselves from the body functions of mere mortals, were said to have sneaked out of their palaces before dawn to defecate in the desert.

The ancient tribe of the Moabites, distantly related to the Hebrews, worshipped several gods including Bel-Phegor or Phegor, the god of dung. Worshippers wishing to make an offering would defecate in front of the altar (it's purely a coincidence that one of the Moabite cities was named Shittim).

According to the Bible, it was God who instructed the Hebrews on sanitation. The modern translation of Deuteronomy 23:12 states, 'You shall have a designated area outside the camp to which you shall go. Included within your tools shall be a spade; when you relieve yourself in this area you shall dig a hole and then cover up your excrement.'

Did you know?

In 2000 a US patent was awarded to a product that used 'colonic gases' to be stored and used to launch a toy missile.

Toilet humour 36

A very attractive woman goes up to the bar in a quiet rural pub and beckons the barman over to her with a sexy wiggle of her finger. He comes over and the woman leans seductively over the bar so her face is just inches from his. She then gently caresses his full beard.

'Are you the landlord?' she asks in a low, sensuous voice, softly stroking his face with both hands.

'Actually, no,' he replies in a faltering voice.

'Well can you get him for me? I need to speak to him,' she says, by now running her hands up beyond his beard and caressing his hair.

'I'm afraid I can't,' stutters the barman, clearly aroused. 'He's not here tonight. Is there anything I can do?'

'Yes there is. I need you to give him a message,' she continues huskily, running her fingers along his lips and into his mouth.

'Tell him that there's no toilet paper in the ladies.'

Bidet controversy!

The first bidets were developed in France in the very early 1700s and were first advertised in Paris in 1739 (the word itself derives from a French word for pony, since sitting astride a bidet was similar to horse riding).

A furniture dealer failed to understand the significance of the device and offered one as a 'porcelain violin case with four legs'.

In Victorian England, where the words 'French' and 'Parisian' carried saucy connotations, the bidet was unacceptable and the very word itself was unmentionable in polite circles.

When the Ritz Carlton Hotel in New York installed bidets in all of its rooms in the early 1900s, self-appointed guardians of public morals were so offended that they forced the hotel to take them all out again.

Flushed with success

A new type of toilet, the 'Pedestal Vase', won a gold medal at the London Health Exhibition of 1884 after successfully demonstrating that in one 2-gallon flush it could successfully clear ten apples averaging 1¼ inches in diameter.

John Shanks (whose company was to later merge with the pottery firm Armitage) patented his first toilet in 1864. At its inaugural test he grabbed the cap from a workman's head and threw it in the bowl just as the chain was pulled. As the cap was successfully flushed away Shanks cried, 'It works!'

Prince or plumber?

In 1871 the Prince of Wales, later King Edward VII, stayed at Londesborough Lodge, near Scarborough. Soon after his return to the royal household at Sandringham, he was struck with typhoid but recovered. Two of his party died, however, including his personal groom and the Earl of Chesterfield. It was obvious that bad sanitation was responsible for the typhoid outbreak and this led the Prince to remark that if he could not be a prince, his next preference would be a plumber.

Cleanliness is next to Godliness

The Romans had three gods to watch after their bathrooms:

CLOACINA was the goddess of the drains and also stools

CREPITUS was the god of toilets and also flatulence

STERCUTIUS was the god of odour (Stercutius was one of Saturn's surnames, given to him when he carpeted the earth with dung to make it fertile)

Toilet humour 37

Little Jimmy's parents were training him to use the toilet but, no matter how hard he tried, Jimmy managed to pee everywhere but in the toilet bowl itself. Frustrated by the lack of progress and the mess, Jimmy's mother decided to take him to the doctor.

After an examination the doctor told her that Jimmy's willy was so small that he had trouble getting a proper grip on it.

'There's nothing I can do medically but I can recommend an old wives' tale. If you give him two slices of unbuttered toast in the morning his willy will grow.'

The following morning, Jimmy jumped out of bed and raced downstairs to the kitchen. On the table were a dozen slices of toast.

'Mummy,' Jimmy said with a confused look, 'The doctor said I only have to eat two pieces of toast.'

'That's right, dear,' his mother replied. 'The other ten are for your dad.'

Don't get lippy!

According to a radio report, a middle school in Birmingham was faced with a unique problem. A number of girls were beginning to use lipstick and would put it on in the school toilets just before home time. While that wasn't a huge problem in itself, after applying their lipstick they would press their lips to the mirror leaving dozens of little lip prints that were really difficult and time-consuming to remove.

Finally, the headmistress decided that something had to be done. She called all the girls into the toilets and met them there with the caretaker. She explained that the lipstick prints were causing a problem for the caretaker who had to stay late each night just to clean them off. To show them how difficult it was to clean the mirrors, she asked the caretaker to demonstrate what he had to do. As all the girls watched he put on rubber gloves and then dipped a rag into one of the toilet bowls. After squeezing out excess toilet water he would wipe away the stains, then squeegee the mirrors clean.

Since then there have been no lip prints on the mirror . . .

Did you know?

The Canaanites were one of several tribes along the Eastern Mediterranean who worshipped dung.

In-flight entertainment

A very drunk Gerard Finneran, the fifty-eight-year-old head of a US investment bank, was travelling first class from Buenos Aires to New York in 1995. After being refused any more alcohol, Finneran became abusive to the airline staff and climbed on top of the beverage trolley where he proceeded to drop his trousers and defecate, using linen napkins as toilet paper. Then, as the airline later stated in court, he began 'tracking faeces throughout the aircraft'. At his trial he was sentenced to three hundred hours of community service and handed a $50,000 cleaning bill. Finneran promised the judge that 'you will never hear of me doing anything like this again'.

Toilet humour 38

A woman is getting ready for bed when she says to her husband, 'Honey, I think my breasts are too small. I'm considering getting implants. What do you reckon?'

The husband shakes his head, 'No, all you have to do is take a piece of toilet tissue and rub it between your breasts twice a day.'

His wife looks surprised and asks, 'You think that's effective?'

The husband replies, 'Sure. It seems to work for your arse.'

Statistically speaking

Fifty-four per cent of Americans fold their toilet tissue neatly before using it, while 35 per cent screw it into a ball.

Caught in the act

Theos Karamani, a Greek midget and part of a criminal gang, was involved in a botched jewellery robbery. He ran into a restaurant, hotly pursued by the police, and then appeared to vanish. Nobody saw him leave so the police searched high and low in the kitchens, in all the storage areas, the freezers, under all the tables – but he was nowhere to be found. It was only when police officer Nikolas Panotis went to the toilet that Karamani was discovered. Panotis lifted the toilet lid and there he was, curled in the bowl.

At first the midget denied he was the wanted man, claiming to be a plumber 'doing complicated repairs'.

WC stands for Water Conservation

Toilets made before 1983 typically used between 4 and 6 gallons of water per flush. New low-flow toilets designed to conserve water use only 1 to 1.3 gallons.

Since the early 1990s, the American city of San Antonio has encouraged its citizens to adopt low-flow toilets, offering subsidies if they turn in their old toilet. These are then crushed and the small ceramic pieces are used to pave nature trails since they reflect light along the paths at night.

Did you know?

For obvious reasons, astronauts are not permitted to eat beans or cabbage before a space flight.

Cesspit concealment

Hearing the approach of a band of noblemen seeking to depose him, King James I of Scotland attempted to hide in a cesspit concealed under his chambers in the Black Monastery in Perth. The traitors, led by Sir Robert Grames, searched the room, which was occupied by the Queen and her maids, but found no sign of the King. Thinking the coast was clear, King James (who was very fat) opened the trapdoor and shouted for the women to help him out. In the process one of the maids fell in on top of the King and the noise alerted Sir Robert. After laughing at the King's predicament he jumped in the cesspit and killed the King, stabbing him sixteen times.

Facts on Farts

- Flatulence produces a mixture of six gases: carbon dioxide, hydrogen, hydrogen sulphide, methane, nitrogen and oxygen.

- The sound of a fart depends on two things: the tightness of the sphincter muscle and the speed of the gas being propelled.

- Farts have been clocked at a speed of 10 feet per second.

- A person produces about half a cubic litre of farts a day distributed over an average of fourteen farts per day.

- The word 'fart' comes from the Old English *feortan*, meaning 'to break wind'.

- Experienced fart lighters recommend the wearing of denim to protect the skin from burns. Cotton clothes are also recommended (dampened if possible) due to their high fire point; at 210°C they are difficult to ignite accidentally. Modern synthetic fibres such as polyester or nylon are not recommended as they can catch fire easily and adhere to the skin. Performing fart lighting with no clothing at all can result in serious burns to the anus or scrotum.

- Flatulence-producing foods include: beans, lentils, dairy products, onions, garlic, leeks, turnips, radishes, potatoes, oats, wheat, cashews and Jerusalem artichokes (or, fartichokes).

- Less than 1 per cent of a fart is made up of the chemicals that stink, but they're so pungent that they can be sniffed despite their low concentration levels.

- The odour of farts comes from small amounts of hydrogen sulphide gas. The more sulphur-rich your diet, the more sulphides will be produced by the bacteria in your gut, and the more your farts will smell. Foods such as cauliflower, eggs and meat are notorious for producing the smelliest farts.

- The top five flatulent animals (in order) are: termites, camels, zebras, sheep and cows.

- Live yoghurt can reduce the occurrence of flatulence.

- Beans contain specific types of sugar molecules that are large and indigestible by the small intestines. They pass on to the large intestines, where colonies of bacteria latch onto them, multiplying rapidly and releasing gases as they do.

Did you know?

In the eighteenth and nineteenth centuries, some well-to-do gentlemen carried hollow walking canes that they could urinate into if they were caught short away from a toilet.

- Help for sufferers of severe farting comes in the form of air-tight undergarments that contain replaceable charcoal filters, or inserts containing activated charcoal that can be worn in regular underwear like pantiliners.

- Suppressing your farts can result in constipation or haemorrhoids.

- Excessive farting can be an indication of Irritable Bowel Syndrome.

- An early example of farting humour in literature appears in the fourteenth-century 'Miller's Tale' by Chaucer. The character Nicholas farts in the face of his rival Absolom: 'This Nicholas anon let fle a fart/As greet as it had been a thunder-dent.'

- Human vegetarians fart more than non-vegetarians.

- Flatulence runs in families because they have a tendency to harbour similar intestinal parasites, along with an inclination to eat the same types of foods.

- The Protestant theologian Martin Luther (1483–1546) suffered terribly from constipation and once boasted that he 'could drive away the evil spirit with a single fart'.

- Few people are aware of one of Thomas Edison's little-known experiments in which he fed an associate large doses of a laxative to see if the resulting flatulence would be able to propel him through the air. It didn't.

- The older you get, the more you fart as your bowel becomes less elastic.

- Research has shown that women fart just as much as men (they just don't make a big scene of it).

Toilet humour **39**

Caller: 'Hello . . . is that the Incontinence Hotline?'
Operator: 'Please hold.'

That's just gross!

- Well-to-do Roman women imported hyena faeces from Africa with which to powder their faces.

It's a tough job . . .

One of the worst jobs in history must have been the Groom of the Stool. In the royal court the role was actually quite prestigious but the task certainly wasn't; the job involved wiping the King's bottom and the role became best known during the reign of Henry VIII. The Tudors believed that their monarchs were appointed by God and, as such, everything had to be done for them – they were far too important to wipe their own backsides. The position was usually granted to a high-ranking aristocrat since only a person with this sort of stature was felt worthy of touching a king's arse.

There were two basic tools of the trade; a lightweight, portable, padded box called the 'close stool' for Henry to sit on (with a bucket or basin strategically placed beneath a hole) and material with which to wipe him. Henry's close stool was elaborate and grand as befitted the King of England. The seat was padded with down, it was covered in black velvet, and decorated with ribbons and fringes and over 2,000 gilt nails – almost resembling a miniature throne. While his subjects were wiping themselves with clumps of moss, Henry used a thick and absorbent cloth woven into a diamond pattern, called diaper cloth (the origin of the American word for a nappy).

Each time Henry VIII evacuated his bowels the 'Royal Stool' was examined in order to check on his well-being. With the crude medical knowledge of the time, the main remedy for any sort of digestive problem was an enema, which was administered by the Groom of the Stool. In September 1539 it was reported with great satisfaction to the King's Secretary, Thomas Cromwell, that after the King had been with administered with a laxative and an enema he had enjoyed a 'very fair siege'.

Despite the nature of the task, the position of Groom of the Stool was very highly paid and was usually a stepping-stone to higher office.

NB While most close stools were disguised as pieces of furniture, or in some recorded cases as stacks of books, some owners were proud to draw attention to their use. In these cases craftsmen worked with inlaid gold and silver, decorated with semi-precious stones. Motifs included birds, animals, landscapes, hunting scenes and even Japanese and Chinese motifs. The seats themselves were usually velvet or leather.

Did you know?

King James I enjoyed hunting so much that he wouldn't leave the saddle even to relieve himself. His servants had a nasty mess to clean up at the end of the day ...

The pee curse

Can urinating in a font be an unlucky omen? Well St Dunstan thought so when King Ethelred (the Unready) was baptized in AD 968. On seeing this happen the man of god predicted the 'slaughter of English people' in his lifetime – a prophecy that came true when the King, in an act of revenge against Viking raids, commanded his forces to massacre all the Danish men, women and children who had settled in England.

> 'All my good reading, you might say, was done in the toilet.
> There are passages in *Ulysses* which can be read only in the
> toilet – if one wants to extract the full flavour of their content.'
>
> HENRY MILLER

Just potty

In the times of chamber pots, a walk along the city streets would often be ruined by unforeseen showers, since it was customary to empty the contents of these pots from upper windows into the gutters below. Some Parisians, however, thought nothing of throwing out the whole pot – inflicting quite serious injury on anyone unfortunate enough to be passing underneath at the same time. Although a ban was imposed on this practice in 1395, it was ignored by most citizens.

Toilet humour **40**

Q: What would get your man to put down the toilet seat?

A: A sex-change operation.

Statistically speaking

The average amount of faeces excreted by a person over seventy years is 2.6 tons.

Doo-doos

The sign of a successful party in the eighteenth century wasn't the number of empties in the bin the next day but the number of broken chamber pots. The host would hire chamber pots for a small fee to accommodate a large number of guests and many ended up broken in the course of drunken behaviour.

King Loo-uis XIV

• King Louis XIV's chamber pot was made from solid gold and decorated with his coat of arms.

• The King thought nothing of greeting visitors or conducting affairs of the state while sitting on the toilet. One courtier commented that he sat on it 'as if it were a throne'.

- An examination after his death revealed that the monarch had an oversize stomach and a bowel twice as large as normal, which might have accounted for the length of time he spent on the royal toilet.

- Men attending royal banquets in the court of King Loius XIV didn't ever have to feel lonely. After dinner (and after women had excused themselves), chamber pots were provided so no one had to leave the company of his fellow guests when it came to relieving himself.

- The King regularly purged his bowels to keep himself healthy. In the last year of his life he had four hundred enemas. So that he wasn't caught short anywhere, the Palace of Versailles had 264 toilets.

- He is said to have conveyed his feelings of admiration for his sister-in-law, the Duchess of Orléans, by farting loudly in her presence.

Did you know?

Because of the stink arising from open sewer gutters running through its streets, nineteenth-century Melbourne in Australia was nicknamed 'Smellbourne'.

Toilet humour 41

A woman sends her clothing out to her local Chinese laundry. When it comes back there are still stains in her knickers. The next week she encloses a note addressed to the cleaners: 'Use more soap on panties'.

The next week she gets her laundry back but there are still stains. Attached is a note that says, 'Use more paper on ass'.

Not in your own back yard

In the seventeenth century, those who lived in the English countryside were advised to relieve themselves 'at least a bow's shot away' from their cottage. This was to prevent waste from seeping into well water near their homes.

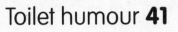

Did you know?

In Ireland and Scotland urine was used as a wool softener in the manufacture of tweed.

Faeces facts

Ever sat there puzzled by your turds? Me too! Here are the answers to a few burning questions:

Why are faeces brown?

The colour comes from iron. Iron in haemoglobin in red blood cells gives blood its red colour, and iron in the waste product bilirubin gives rise to its brown colour. A lot of it ends up in the intestine, where it is further modified by bacterial action.

Why does corn on the cob still look like corn on the cob when you excrete it?

Well, what you see in the toilet bowl isn't actually the original corn kernel – it's just the outer coating. Made from cellulose, it's indigestible and passes through the intestines untouched, only to emerge looking like the whole kernel.

Why so some turds float and others sink?

It's down to their gas content. Sometimes the gases produced by bacteria in the gut end up dispersed throughout the turd, which makes them 'floaters'.

What's in faeces?

Three-quarters of the average turd is water. Of the remaining portion, approximately one-third is composed of dead bacteria, one-third is indigestible substances known as fibre and the remaining portion is a mixture of mucus from the lining of the intestine, dead cells, fats, phosphates, live bacteria and protein.

Why 'poop'?

It's believed that the word 'poop' comes from the Middle English word *poupon* or *popen*, which originally meant 'fart' (the word being onomatopoeic). The shift in meaning to 'excretion' is thought to have happened around 1900.

Did you know?

Chastity belts once featured small holes to allow the release of waste. However, in many cases it was almost impossible to keep the devices clean, with the result that many women, unable to bear the smell and discomfort, committed suicide.

International Rescue

If you ever find yourself caught short in Croatia or bursting in Bulgaria, here is how to ask 'Where's the toilet?' in different languages.

Afrikaans	Wār is die toilet?
Albanian	Ku është banjoja?
Arabic (Modern Standard)	Ayn al-ḥammām?
Armenian (Eastern)	Vortegh e zugarane?

Bulgarian ....Kade e toaletnata?)

Chinese (Mandarin)........Cèsuǒ zài nǎli? *or* Xǐshǒujiān zài nǎli?

Croatian ....Gdje je zahod?

Czech ....Kde je prosím záchod?

Danish ....Hvor er toilettet?

Dutch ....Wār is de WC? *or* Wār is het toilet?

Estonian..........................Kus on tualett?

Flemish ....Waor is 't gemak?

Fijian ....E vei na vale-lailai?

Finnish ....Missä on vessa?

French ....Où sont les toilettes?

German ....Wo ist die Toilette?

Greek..............................Pu íne i tualéta?

Hawaiian.........................Aia i hea ka lua?

Hebrew ....Eifo ha'sheirutim?

Hindi ....Tāyalet kahan hai?

Hungarian........................Hol van a mosdó?

Icelandic.........................Hvar er klósettið?

Indonesian......................Di manakah kamar kecil?

Italian..............................Dov'è la toilette? *or* Dov'è il bagno?

Japanese........................Benjo wa doko desu ka

Korean ....Hwajangsiri eodiyeyo

Latvian............................Kur ir tualete?

Lithuanian.......................Kur yra tualetas?

Luxembourgish ....Wou ass d'Toilette?

Maltese...........................Fejn it-tojlit?

Māori ....Kei hea te wharepaku?

Mongolian.......................Biye zasakh gazar khaana baidag ve?

Nepali ....Sauchalaya kata chha

154

Norwegian ....Hvor er toalettet? (Bokmål), Kvar er toalettet? (Nynorsk)

Polish ....Gdzie jest toaleta?

Portuguese ....Onde é a casa de banho / o banheiro?

Romanian ....Unde este toaleta?

Russian ....Gde tualet?

Serbian ....Gde je toalet'?

Slovenian ....Kje imate stranišče?

Spanish ....¿Dónde están los aseos? *or* ¿Dónde están los sanitarios?

Swahili ....Choo kiko wapi?

Swedish ....Var är toaletten?

Thai ....Hôrng náhm yòo têe năi?

Turkish ....Tuvalet nerede?

Ukrainian ....De tualet?

Urdu ....Bayt-ul-khala khana kahan hay?

Vietnamese...................Cầu tiêu ở đâu?

Welsh ....Ble mae'r toiled

Zulu ....Likuphi ikamelo lokugezela?

Statistically speaking

According to a survey conducted among UK women in 2010, the most annoying male habit were leaving the toilet seat up (54 per cent). The next most annoying habits were leaving damp towels on the bed (23 per cent) and dumping dirty laundry on the floor (15 per cent).

Toilet humour 42

A woman has been taken on a first date to a very exclusive restaurant. The onion soup is really rich and she immediately feels a gurgling in her stomach. As the waiter is clearing the dishes she lets rip an enormous fart. Trying to save face, she says to the waiter, 'Sir! Would you please stop that immediately.'

Without missing a beat the waiter replies, 'Certainly, madam. Did you notice which way it was headed?'

Standard procedure

The British Standard BS6465, Part 1 (1984) provides a scale of the minimum requirements in the provision of sanitary appliances in public places. According to the Standard, two hundred men visiting theatres or concert venues need just one WC between them but four urinals, whereas the same number of men at a cinema need three WCs and only two urinals. Go figure!

> 'Today you can go to the gas station and find the cash
> register open and the toilets locked.
> They must think toilet paper is worth more than money.'
>
> JOEY BISHOP

Bog blast

In 2004, Hanley town centre in Stoke-on-Trent was rocked by the sound of an exploding Superloo. The blast was so fierce that it ripped the whole roof off and lifted the surrounding pavement. Fortunately no one was inside at the time. The incident was blamed on a fault in high voltage cables running beneath the toilet.

A spokesman later commented, 'This could have been quite distressing, if not dangerous, if someone had been in there.'

Necessity is the mother of invention

A device patented in 1988 by inventor Timothy Probasco of Baltimore, Maryland automatically closes the seat when the toilet is flushed. As the patent application states, 'Adults, particularly women, have complained for years that men users of toilets leave the toilet seat of a toilet in an upright position. At times, women users of a toilet have rushed into the bathroom and have fallen into the commode with a shocking splash.'

Fellow inventor Burton Axelrod of Girard, Pennsylvania, patented the 'Shit Zapper' in 1986; a device that microwaved turds into ashes than could be easily disposed of without the need for water.

Did you know?

The most famous toilet paper was once the Sears Roebuck catalogue which combined great toilet reading material with a ready supply of toilet tissue. Its use declined rapidly when colour printing was introduced; the inks made the paper non-absorbent.

Enema of the State . . .

All you've ever wanted to know about colon cleansing . . .

• The concept of colon cleansing dates back to the ancient Egyptians, who believed that most diseases were related to the diet. Regularly binging with laxatives was recommended to stay healthy (some of these purgings lasted up to three consecutive days).

• King Louis XIV is said to have had two thousand enemas which many believe were responsible for his long, healthy life (he died aged seventy-seven).

• The Victorians believed that 'autointoxication', the process of being poisoned by your own faeces, was a serious medical problem, best combated with regular and strong enemas. Getting rid of bodily waste almost became an obsession among mothers and nursemaids – so much so that in many cases, enemas became mixed up in a child's mind with sex. The result was that the act of purging one's body became almost eroticized, and was soon known by the euphemism of 'Victorian discipline'.

- A bus driver in Bulgaria was prescribed a paprika enema (you can guess what happened next . . .) The pain and the burning sensation were so acute that he was unable to sit down for a week and sued for loss of earnings.

- Mae West said she had an enema and an orgasm every day, but failed to mention whether the two were in any way related.

- According to a former LA County Prosecutor investigating the death of Marilyn Monroe, the star was killed by a barbiturate enema.

- The so-called Enema Bandit attacked several women in the Chicago area in 1966, breaking into their houses to rob them, then administering an enema at gunpoint before he left. In one attack he broke into a college dorm where five girls were asleep. He administered four enemas but locked the fifth girl in a wardrobe after telling her she was too ugly. It was rumoured that she had to drop out of school and received psychological counselling to recover from such cruelty. The Enema Bandit became the subject of Frank Zappa's song 'The Illinois Enema Bandit'.

- A former maid of Michael Jackson claimed the singer used an enema every day for pleasure rather than weight loss.

Toilet humour 43

A man gets on a bus and sits next to an elderly lady. A few minutes into the journey he lets loose a long, noisy fart. Embarrassed, he tries to make conversation, turning to his neighbour to ask, 'Do you by any chance have today's paper?'

The lady frowns at him and replies, 'No, but the next time we pass by a tree I'll lean out of the window and grab you a handful of leaves.'

Statistically speaking

According to the Xinhua news agency, more than 3 million Chinese regularly drink their own urine, believing the practice strengthens the immune system, improving health and longevity.

Going in style

Still to catch on in the West, about half the homes in Japan feature a Washlet toilet, which combines a toilet with the features of a bidet. Resembling a conventional toilet, the Washlet cleans the user using a spray of warm water and then dries with a jet of warm air, which, supporters claim, is far more effective and hygienic than using toilet paper.

The water nozzle emerges from underneath the toilet seat and has two settings, one for washing the bottom and one for what is known euphemistically as 'feminine cleaning'. The nozzle itself doesn't make contact with the user and it's self-cleaning. Additional features include seat heating, massage options, automatic lid opening and automatic flushing. And if that's not enough, before you leave the bathroom it can even freshen the air. Some Washlet models allow the water temperature and water pressure to be adjusted to match the user's personal preferences. High-end Washlets can also provide vibrating and pulsating jets of water, claimed by manufacturers to be beneficial for constipation and haemorrhoids. The most advanced models can play music to relax the sphincter and can cost over £3,000.

One very sophisticated Washlet takes your blood pressure while you're sitting down, and even analyses the content of your urine. If you so wish, it will also email the results to your doctor!

Find your way in life

Outhouses were usually positioned a long way from the house to prevent smells or contamination, which meant in pre-electricity days they were hard to find in the dark. To get round this problem, homeowners usually connected a long piece of string from the main building to the outhouse so all you had to do was hold on to the string and follow it. An added benefit was that the string doubled up as a clothes line.

Did you know?

Jack Nicholson used to have a toilet seat with a rattlesnake embedded in it.

Lav Nav

This battery-powered device attaches to any toilet and, using a built-in infrared sensor, illuminates the toilet and its surroundings as you approach so you don't need to turn on the often dazzling main light. And to avoid any bleary-eyed middle-of-the-night accidents, green and red lights also indicate whether the seat is up or down. At the time of writing the device costs £20.

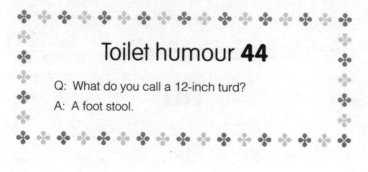

Toilet humour 44

Q: What do you call a 12-inch turd?
A: A foot stool.

Statistically Speaking

The toilet handle in a public bathroom can have up to forty thousand germs per square inch.

In space no one can hear you fart

Ever wondered how astronauts deal with waste in weight-lessness?

- During lift-off and landing, astronauts wear what is basically a 'space nappy', or Maximum Absorbency Garment (MAG), under their space suits. Once in space, they use what you or I would recognize as a toilet – albeit a very sophisticated and expensive one.

- To reduce the need to defecate in space, astronauts undergo pre-launch bowel clearing and stick to a diet low in fibre.

- Remaining seated in acceleration couches before lift-off isn't a comfortable time for many astronauts – not just because they're on their backs with their legs elevated, but because this position increases blood flow to the kidneys, which respond by increasing the producing of urine. Maintaining this position in the hours before launch will fill the bladder to capacity.

- The first US astronaut in space, Alan Shepard, encountered this problem on his 1961 flight. This was before the advent of the MAG and, rather than abort the mission, Shepard was advised to urinate in his space suit. Secured in a capsule with his feet in the air Shepard felt the urine slowly make its way down his body towards his head, hoping that it wouldn't reach this far, or cause any electrical shorts in the wires of his spacesuit. Fortunately, it settled without harm in an area behind his back. The event was humorously depicted in the movie *The Right Stuff*.

- In the zero gravity environment of space, it's possible to move oneself around the cabin of a spacecraft by farting. Restraining devices on space toilets aren't just there to secure an airtight seal on the seat, they also prevent astronauts from being thrust away in the case of flatulence.

- During the flight of *Apollo 8*, Commander Frank Borman awoke feeling ill. After vomiting twice he suffered a bout of diarrhoea that left the spacecraft full of small globules of vomit and faeces, which his two crew members had to clean up.

- The toilet onboard *Skylab* was as sophisticated as the space station itself. Rather than rely on water it used air pressure – thus avoiding the problem of defecating in zero gravity. The astronauts would secure themselves to the 'Super John' with a seat belt, handholds and foot restraints. Once in position, a jet of air directed at the bottom would help loosen and separate the waste. A second blast of air would flush the waste into a holding tank.

- The most expensive toilet in the world is actually one that's out of this world – onboard the International Space Station. Russian-built, it cost $19 million in 2007 and was, according to NASA, a bargain compared to the cost of developing and building one from scratch.

- Solid waste can't be jettisoned into space since it might collide with a space station or spacecraft. The ejection of urine, too, isn't without its problems. In space it vaporizes into a fog-like cloud that can block the astronauts' view and prevent clear photography of Earth and space.

Did you know?

Emperor Napoleon III of France suffered from diarrhoea. When he commanded his forces at the Battle of Sedan in 1870 he had towels stuffed down his breeches acting as Emperor-sized nappies.

Toilet humour 45

A husband and wife were in a bar, sitting next to a drunk. Suddenly the drunk gets up, shouts 'Listen to this!' then farts loudly.

The wife is extremely offended and the angry husband grabs the drunk and says, 'You're disgusting! You just farted before my wife.'

The drunk shrugs and replies, "I'm sorry. I didn't know it was her turn."

'Well, I don't use the toilet much to pee in.
I almost always pee in the yard or the garden,
because I like to pee on my estate.'

IGGY POP

Urine: some curious customs

- The Siberian Chukchi community, who inhabit the Bering Sea area of the Arctic Ocean, had some strange habits. Tradition once required them to offer their wives for sex to a male visitor, but only after he had drunk her urine to show he was worthy of the honour.

- Women in ancient Greece and Rome used to drink turpentine to make their urine smell of roses. This is not to be recommended since, at best, drinking turps can cause severe abdominal pain and, at worse, loss of vision and kidney failure.

- Courtesans in sixteenth-century Venice used to soak their hair in urine and sit in the sun to develop bright reddish-gold hair.

- Captain John G. Bourke of the Third Cavalry reported in 1881 that he witnessed the Zuni Indians of Mexico perform their ritual Urine Dance, so-called because it is preceded by drinking from a 2-gallon container of human urine. His written report describes this as a 'disgusting rite' and a 'vile ceremony'.

- It wasn't fun living in a superstitious family in eighteenth-century Scotland. On New Year's Day, the lady of the house would sprinkle urine on her sleeping family in the belief that this would protect them.

- According to an old wives' tale, if you soaked a man's socks in your urine he would fall in love with you.

- The Hottentot tribe of South Africa had a peculiar marriage blessing. The men of the village formed an inner circle while the women formed an outer ring. When everyone was sitting comfortably the priest would go to the groom and urinate over him, then would do the same to the bride. At the same time he would pronounce, 'May you live long and happily together. May you have a son before the end of the year. May this son live to be a comfort to you in your old age.' The blessing ended when the priest had emptied his bladder.

That's just gross!

☞ **The Nuer tribe in Ethiopia wash themselves with cow urine.**

The Great Stink

If you lived or worked in London in June 1858 you couldn't help but notice the disgusting smell that hung across the whole city. That month it was so hot and dry that the current of the Thames slowed almost to a stop, meaning the sewage that flowed daily into the river stayed put, putrefying in the heat.

The time became known as the Great Stink; the Thames was soon awash with human and animal faeces, dead dogs and cats, entrails from the nearby slaughterhouses, rotten food and the effluent of countless factories. It was described by the Prime Minister the Earl of Derby as 'a Stygian pool reeking with ineffable and unbearable horror'.

Londoners invested in scented handkerchiefs to mask the smell, while politicians in the Houses of Parliament, located on the banks of the river, ordered curtains soaked in chloride of lime to be hung to similarly obscure the stench.

After two weeks of misery and the danger of a cholera outbreak the rains came, the Thames began to flow again and the smell began to dissipate. Shortly after that Parliament, shocked into action, authorized £3 million to develop a massive sewer system for London. Over the next seven years over 13,000 miles of pipes were laid to channel London's waste downstream away from the capital.

The toilet paper caper

According to employees at the Marshall County Courthouse in Iowa, in early 2007 toilet paper started disappearing from the women's restroom at an unusually high rate. This continued for a while before a brazen thirty-eight-year-old thief was caught in the act taking three rolls of two-ply toilet paper from a courthouse storage cupboard.

The offence would have been classed as a 'misdemeanour fifth-degree theft', usually resulting in less than a year behind bars. However, court officials had considered charging the offender on a per-roll basis, which meant she would have faced three years of incarceration for the three rolls of toilet paper. In the end she was declared incompetent to stand trial.

The name of the thief? Suzanne Butts.

Did you know?

An old German euphemism for the toilet was the 'plumsklo' – literally the 'plop closet'.

From false teeth to hamsters ...

According to a survey carried out by American Standard, the leading manufacturer of toilets in the US, these are some of the items that people have witnessed being flushed (or being attempted to be flushed) down their toilets: false teeth, goldfish, socks, hamsters, mice, toy cars, rubber ducks, action figures, Barbie dolls, underwear, bras, T-shirts, shoes, jewellery and entire rolls of toilet paper.

Toilet humour 46

A cowboy is sitting in an outhouse when he hears a noise from below. Surprised, he looks down and there's a Native American looking up at him.

'Jesus!' he exclaims in surprise. 'How long have you been hiding there?'

The Indian replies, 'Many moons.'

Slash and grab!

The natural place to put your handbag while using a public toilet is to hang it from the hook on the back of the door – a fact known to thieves in New Jersey who targeted women by reaching over the door to grab the bags and then running off. To counter the thefts the city removed the hooks from the doors. Enterprising thieves then replaced them.

In 1991 New York fell victim to a thief with a very specific target: the handles of the city's public toilets. In a short space of time 109 toilet handles were stolen including one from a toilet down the hallway from the office of the then Mayor, David Dinkins. The city's spokesman, Lisa Ryan, commented that, apart from a tiny amount of brass in each handle, they had no commercial value. She added, 'Maybe he's refurbishing and reselling them . . . I don't know why anyone would want them.'

It was later suggested that the thief was selling them on the brown market . . .

Statistically Speaking

The first toilet cubicle as you enter a public bathroom is likely to be the least used and therefore the cleanest.

You're never too young to learn

Seventeenth- and eighteenth-century British upper classes, in an attempt to make their children more accomplished, used to put inexpensive collections of poems and verse in their bathroom for use as toilet paper. The idea was that the child could learn a few stanzas before the paper was put to its alternative use.

Did you know?

It's tradition for Russian cosmonauts to urinate on the tyre of the bus that will transport them to the launch pad (one assumes they do this before donning their spacesuits). This strange custom originated with their former comrade Yuri Gagarin, the first man in space.

In the navy

Most people have heard of the SEALs, the elite US Navy commandoes. A much lower profile group is the Shit Patrol, the (unofficial) name given to a special team of enlisted men responsible for keeping a ship's sewage system clean and unobstructed (for those who want to know, toilets are flushed with salt water and the waste is pumped out into open seas).

Did you know?

The Klingon for 'Where is the toilet?' is 'nuqDaq 'oH puchpa''e?'

I won't be a minute ...

There's spending a long time on the toilet and there's spending a *really* long time on the toilet. Then there's spending two years. In February 2008, police from Ness County in Kansas were called to a house by a thirty-six-year-old man worried about the state of health of his girlfriend. Arriving, they found a thirty-five-year-old woman stuck to the toilet seat, not due to superglue or because she was tied, but because her own skin had actually grown around the seat itself – the result of being seated there for two years.

Initially refusing any medical assistance, the unnamed woman was eventually persuaded by police and her boyfriend to visit a hospital. 'We pried the toilet seat off and the seat went with her to the hospital,' said Ness County Sheriff Brian Whipple. 'The hospital removed it.'

According to her boyfriend the woman had gone to the bathroom but had refused to leave. He would bring her food and water but every time he asked her to come out her reply was, 'Maybe tomorrow.' When police entered the bathroom they found her disoriented with her sweat pants down to her mid-thigh. At the time of the report the woman refused to cooperate with doctors or the police and it was uncertain whether any charges would be brought against her boyfriend who couldn't explain why it had taken him two years to raise the alarm.

Statistically Speaking

The Pentagon gets through 636 rolls of toilet paper a day.

Be our guest

To reassure guests, hotels fold the last sheet of toilet paper into a small triangle or 'V' shape as a sign that their room has been serviced and that no one has used the toilet since it was cleaned. Though as it's been pointed out, it's also a sign that a complete stranger has had their hands all over the toilet paper before you.

Toilet humour 47

Q: Did you hear about the couple that were wed in a public toilet?

A: It was a marriage of convenience.

There's something about Mary

In 2009 Cameron Diaz told Jay Leno on *The Tonight Show* about her own policy on water conservation; she flushes only when she has to, adhering to the adage, 'If it's yellow leave it mellow. If it's brown flush it down.'

Did you know?

It's thought that the first flushing toilets were used in Crete as early as 2000 BC.

Blar humbug!

In many Middle Eastern cultures and also in India, only the left hand is used for wiping yourself. It's a strict taboo to accept, offer or eat food with this hand. A way of remembering is the acronym BLAR: for any bodily functions Below the belly button (i.e. excretion), use the Left. For anything Above it (i.e. eating and drinking), use the Right.

That tickles!

In the fifteenth and sixteenth centuries the British upper classes used to wipe their bottoms with goose feathers attached to a pliable holder. The sixteenth-century French writer Rabelais satirized this custom, writing that one of his characters, Gargantua, improved his grip by having the feathers still attached to the goose's neck.

174

Putting rejection behind you

If you're an author or would-be author there's nothing more annoying and depressing than getting the familiar rejection letter from publishers or agents. The instinctive reaction is to wipe your backside on it – well, now you can. If you send a rejection letter to lulu.com they'll print it on quality toilet tissue, replicating the text throughout the whole roll.

Catharsis doesn't come cheap though. It's currently £60 for four rolls (the minimum order) . . . although it's cheaper than therapy.

> 'Men who consistently leave the toilet seat up secretly want women to get up to go the bathroom in the middle of the night and fall in.'
>
> RITA RUDNER

Download then download

Available at around £55 the US-manufactured iCarta combines an iPod dock with a toilet roll holder. The manufacturers claim it will 'enhance your experience in the smallest room' and features four integrated moisture-resistant speakers to deliver 'exceptional clarity and high quality sound'. Mains-powered, the device also charges your iPod when it's in the dock. Now that's rock 'n' roll.

Toilet humour 48

A teacher told her class to tell her what they did at the weekend.

Janey said, 'I went to see my nanna.'

The teacher said, 'That's lovely but you're old enough to use grown-up words. Next time, Janey, say, "I went to see my grandma."'

Laura said, 'I went for a ride in my daddy's new brum-brum.'

This time the teacher said, 'How exciting, but remember to use grown-up words. Say, "I went for a ride in my daddy's new car."'

Next it was Stuart's turn. 'I read a whole book by myself, miss.'

'And what was the book called?' asked the teacher.

Stuart replied, 'Winnie the Shit.'

I spy . . .

The CIA were said to have reached the heights of espionage success when they stole one of Nikita Khrushchev's turds during his 1959 visit to the US. After a thorough scientific analysis they concluded that he was in excellent health for a man of his age and portliness.

> **Did you know?**
>
> It is alleged that Winston Churchill was born in a ladies' toilet in Blenheim Palace, Oxfordshire. When asked about the truth of this rumour, Churchill is quoted as saying, 'Although present on that occasion, I have no clear recollection of the events leading up to it.'

Piss artist

John Cousins, a New Zealand music lecturer, had a show with a difference. Called Membrane, this seven-hour performance involved Mr Cousins drinking eighteen to twenty mouthfuls of water at a time and then urinating on a series of rubber membranes to create drum-like sounds. 'I am', he said, 'the biological material in the work.'

When asked about his oeuvre Mr Cousins commented that the inspiration for Membrane comes from the simplest of sources – the sound of dripping water heard in a New Zealand canyon.

Statistically Speaking

There are thirty-five bathrooms in the White House but seventy-eight in Buckingham Palace.

Instructions for use

The first public convenience with flushable toilets opened in London on 2 February 1852. It was a 'Gents' and women had to wait a further nine days to get a version of their very own. The installations were called Public Waiting Rooms, and so novel was the idea that fifty thousand leaflets were distributed to explain what they were for and how they should be used.

> 'If they had told me I was the janitor and would have to mop up and clean the toilets after the show in order to play, I probably would have done it.'
>
> BRUCE SPRINGSTEEN

What makes a Real Man?

According to an article in *GQ* magazine about what characterizes a thirty-year-old man, attributes included making love at least 1,248 times with a minimum of nineteen partners, having a one-night stand he was ashamed of, spending a night in a jail, a brothel, a monastery and a youth hostel . . . and knowing how to clear a blocked toilet.

Toilet humour 49

Q: What's the difference between roast beef and pea soup?

A: Anyone can roast beef.

The Secret Diary of Albert Speer aged 43¾

Albert Speer, Hitler's architect, was imprisoned after the Nuremberg trials and kept a secret diary written on pieces of toilet paper which he then hid in his shoes until sections could be safely smuggled out. He was released after twenty years and the twenty-five thousand pieces of toilet paper were reassembled into his book, *Spandau: The Secret Diaries*.

Did you know?

Early toilet roll holders were far more elaborate than anything you can buy today; some included a roll of paper, a bracket for a candle or oil lamp, a box for matches and a striker, a mirror, a towel hook and an ashtray.

Better decisions from a full bladder

According to psychologists from the University of Twente in the Netherlands, people make more sensible decisions once their bladders are full. This is because the self-control mechanism in the brain that prevents you from going to the toilet until you're ready also exercises restraint across all decision-making faculties, leading to better judgement.

Trapped wind!

In 2007 a man endured four days in darkness in a freezing toilet at his local bowling club, after becoming accidentally locked in. Fifty-five-year-old David Leggatt spent sixteen hours of each day in complete darkness with no food, no heating, no mobile phone and no idea when help would reach him. He survived by drinking water from the tap and kept warm by filling the basin with hot water and immersing his feet to dissipate heat through his body, a tip he learned at a survival course.

Leggatt became a prisoner in the Aberdeen club on a Monday night when the door handle jammed. He gave up crying for help when it was apparent that there was no one around to hear him. It wasn't until Thursday morning when the cleaner arrived and heard his shouts that he was freed. She told reporters, 'Nobody looked for David. A wife may have wondered where he was but he's not married.'

David was philosophical about this bathroom captivity: 'I regret I didn't get trapped behind the bar,' he said, 'but at least I had a toilet.'

Did you know?

Although the first flushing toilet was invented in England in 1596 it wasn't until the 1770s that people started installing them in their homes.

Toilet rolls of the future ...

The first tube-free toilet paper went on sale in the US in October 2010. The brand, Scott Naturals, was introduced to help prevent wastage. According to the manufacturers, Kimberly-Clark, the 17 billion cardboard tubes produced annually in the US account for £160 million-worth of rubbish. In addition to helping the environment, customers will get the added bonus of being able to use every square, right down to the last one, which will no longer be glued to the customary tube.

Although the new brand is being launched in the north-east United States, if it sells well it will expand nationally and then possibly worldwide. A global roll-out, you could say . . .

That's just gross!

Elvis Presley's mother Gladys would urinate into a jar and then add the urine to a glass of beer with an eyedropper in the belief that it offered health benefits.

Toilet humour **50**

Keith goes into a public toilet and sees a man standing in front of the urinal with no arms. Keith takes a leak and, as he's standing there, wonders how the poor guy next to him manages.

As Keith turns to leave, the armless man asks him if he can help him. Being a Good Samaritan Keith agrees.

The man is extremely grateful and asks, 'Can you undo my zip?'

Keith agrees and does what he's asked.

Then the man says, 'Can you reach into my trousers and find your way into my pants?'

Keith shrugs and does this.

'Can you pull my old fella out for me?' the man asks.

Keith pulls it out and sees that it's covered in scabs, rashes, scars and a horrible green mould – and smells like rotting fruit.

The man asks Keith to point it at the urinal. He relieves himself, then asks Keith to shake it, tuck it back in and zip him up again.

Keith does all this and the man says, 'Thanks buddy. I really appreciate that.'

Keith says, 'No problem, I'm glad to help out. But I must ask, what the hell's wrong with your penis?'

The man pulls both his arms out of his jacket and says, 'I've got no idea, but there's no way I'm touching it!'

Sound advice

Many Japanese women are embarrassed about being heard by others while they use public bathrooms and traditionally mask the sound of their bodily functions by flushing the toilet continually, wasting a huge amount of water in the process. To prevent this, a device was introduced in the 1980s that electronically recreates the sound of a flushing toilet. Called the Sound Princess, the device is operated by pushing a button or waving a hand in front of a sensor and it's now routinely placed in new public toilets, and in upgraded older ones. The sound either ends after a preset time or can be halted by a second press on the button. It is estimated that the Sound Princess saves up to 20 litres of water each time it's used.

'The toilets at a local police station have been stolen.
Police say they have nothing to go on.'
RONNIE BARKER

Toilet paper trivia

- We use an average of 8.6 sheets of toilet paper each time we go to the loo.

- Sixty per cent of people look at their toilet paper after they've wiped.

- The US military used toilet paper to camouflage their tanks in Saudi Arabia during Operation Desert Storm in 1991.

- The average person uses 100 rolls of toilet paper each year.

- The first ever toilet paper was used by Chinese emperors in the 1390s. Each sheet measured 2' × 3'.

- Nowadays a standard sheet of toilet paper is 4.5 square inches.

- Approximately 70–75 per cent of the world's population does not use toilet paper.

- Seven per cent of Americans steal rolls of toilet paper from hotels or motels.

- The average amount of toilet paper that one person uses in their lifetime is the equivalent of 384 trees.

- The first coloured toilet paper (introduced in 1957) was pink.

- One-third of all Americans flush the toilet while they are still sitting on it.

- cheap-chic-weddings.com held a contest to find the best wedding dress made from toilet paper.

- White is the most popular colour for toilet paper in the UK, followed by pink and then peach.

- 'Toilegami' is the art of toilet paper origami.

- Today there are over five thousand companies manufacturing toilet paper around the world.

- To supply all the toilet paper required in the world requires a production output of 2.7 rolls per second.

- The average toilet roll is nearly 340 feet long.

- In 1996, President Clinton passed the 'Toilet Paper Law' taxing each roll 6 cents and increasing the price of the product to 30 cents per roll.

- The first advertisements for quality toilet paper in the US implied that inferior products could be responsible for rectal disease.

- When toilet paper first became popular in the mid-1800s it was still considered a taboo subject. Customers, especially women, would whisper their requirements to the storeowner, who usually kept his stock under the counter. A device called Madam's Double Utility Fan, a toilet-tissue holder shaped like a fan, was used to carry the paper discreetly.

- The oldest brand of toilet paper in the US was introduced in 1902. Called Waldorf, it was named after the fashionable Waldorf-Astoria hotel in New York.

- Until the end of the 1800s newspaper and magazines in the US refused to carry advertisements for toilet paper, considering them to be offensive and distasteful. The first ad appeared in the magazine *Atlantic Monthly* in 1890 and just featured a single small picture of the packaging; no marketing copy was allowed. Up until then, promotion of toilet paper brands consisted of leaflets available where the product was stocked.

- Toilet paper can be a good indicator of the strength of the economy. Since shoppers are literally flushing toilet-paper money away, an increase in sales from one-ply to two-ply, or from two-ply to three-ply reveals important clues about the financial health of shoppers and the economy as a whole.

Questions you've always wanted to ask

Can I eat a urinal cake?

In a word, no, unless you want to die painfully. Modern urinal cakes, the deodorizing mints also called 'piss cakes' or 'piss pucks', are mainly paradichlorobenzene. The lethal dosage for this substance for rats is 500 mg/kg when taken orally. So a urine cake weighing 3 ounces (approximately 85 g) eaten by a person weighing 11 stone (approximately 70 kg) would mean a dosage of 1,215 mg/kg – over twice the lethal dose for rats.

Symptoms of paradichlorobenzene poisoning include burning of the mouth, breathing problems, coughing, headaches, slurred speech, jaundice, abdominal pain, nausea, vomiting and diarrhoea.

Did you know?

By 1878 Paris had a network of sewers 360 miles long and people enjoyed taking tours through them in carts pushed by workers and later, small boats.

Toilet humour 51

Little Timmy has been potty trained and the day comes for him to use the big toilet just like his daddy. He pushes up the lid and the seat and, standing on tiptoes, can just about balance his little penis on the rim. Halfway through, the toilet seat slams down and Timmy lets out a horrifying scream.

Not knowing what has happened his worried mother comes rushing upstairs to find her son in the bathroom screaming his head off and clutching his groin.

Looking up at her with his tearstained face he sobs, 'P-p-p-please k-k-k-k-kiss it better.'

His mother folds her arms and sighs, saying, 'Listen, son, don't start your father's shit with me!'

What a way to go

Mystery surrounds the death of early Hollywood film actress Lupe Vélez, who committed suicide in Beverly Hills on 13 December 1944. Rumour has it that at the time of her death Vélez was depressed because her lover, whose child she was carrying, refused to leave his wife and marry her. Leaving a suicide note she took an overdose of barbiturates but instead of killing her they made her violently ill and she rushed to her bathroom to be sick. Leaning over the toilet she passed out and drowned in the toilet bowl.

The events inspired a 1965 film by Andy Warhol entitled *Lupe*.

Answers

Privy Playtime: Toilet **TRUE** or **FALSE**?

1) TRUE	7) FALSE	13) TRUE
2) FALSE	8) TRUE	14) FALSE
3) FALSE	9) FALSE	15) TRUE
4) TRUE	10) TRUE	16) FALSE
5) FALSE	11) FALSE	
6) TRUE	12) TRUE	

Privy Playtime: **CLOSET SUDOKU**

3	2	5	7	6	9	1	4	8
4	9	7	8	1	2	6	5	3
1	8	6	5	3	4	9	7	2
6	1	9	4	2	8	5	3	7
5	3	2	1	7	6	4	8	9
7	4	8	9	5	3	2	6	1
9	5	3	6	8	1	7	2	4
2	7	4	3	9	5	8	1	6
8	6	1	2	4	7	3	9	5

Privy Playtime: **FIND THE POET**

T. S. Eliot

Privy Playtime: **TOILET MAZE**

Privy Playtime: **LOO QUIZ**

1. Gloomy
2. Sloop
3. Aloof
4. Looting
5. Igloo
6. Loony
7. Vindaloo
8. Flood
9. Loofah
10. Saloon
11. Loop
12. Hullabaloo
13. Heirloom
14. Onlooker
15. Floor
16. Doubloon
17. Looseleaf
18. Loophole
19. Bloomers
20. Blood

Sources

Aman, Reinhold, *Talking Dirty* (Robson Books. 1993)

Beadle, Jeremy, *Today's The Day* (W H Allen, 1979)

Booker, James E., *The Vile File* (Headline, 1994)

Bourke, John G., *Scatalogic Rites of All Nations* (1891)

Crombie, David, *The World's Stupidest Laws* (Michael O'Mara Books, 2000)

Davies, A. H., *Thunder, Flash & Thomas Crapper* (Michael O'Mara, 1997)

Eveleigh, David, *Bogs, Baths and Basins* (Sutton Publishing, 2002)

Frauenfelder, Mark, *The World's Worst* (Chronicle Books, 2005)

Garbage, Greta, *Greta Garbage's Outrageous Bathroom Book* (Ten Speed Press, 2001) and *That's Disgusting!* (Ten Speed Press, 1999)

Hobbs, J. and Couzens, T., *Pees and Queues* (Spearhead Press, 1999)

Horan, Julie, *Sitting Pretty* (Robson Books, 1998)

John, A. and Blake, S., *The World's Stupidest Deaths* (Michael O'Mara Books, 2005)

Lambton, Lucinda *Temples of Convenience* (Tempus, 2007)

McGiffin, Carol and Leigh, Mark, *Celebrities Behaving Badly* (Summersdale, 2009)

Owen, Kelly, *Laugh On The Loo* (Marks and Spencer, 2009)

Paschall, J. and Lyon, R., *Odd Laws* (Harper Collins, 1996)

Raum, Elizabeth, *The Story Behind Toilets* (Raintree, 2009)

Robinson, Tony, *The Worst Jobs in History* (Pan Books, 2005)

Shaw, Karl, *Gross* (Virgin Books, 1993) and *Mammoth Book of Tasteless Lists* (Robinson Books, 1998)

Spignessi, Stephen, *The Odd Index*, (Plume Books, 1994)

Sussman, Paul, *Death by Spaghetti* (Fourth Estate, 1996)

Williams, Alan and Noach, Maggie, *The Dictionary of Disgusting Facts* (Futura, 1986)

Wright, Lawrence, *Clean & Decent* (Routledge & Kegan Paul, 1980)